Animals Matter

Books by Marc Bekoff

AUTHOR/COAUTHOR

Animals Matter (2007)
*The Emotional Lives of Animals: A Leading Scientist Explores
  Animal Joy, Sorrow, and Empathy—and Why They Matter* (2007)
*Animal Passions and Beastly Virtues: Reflections on Redecorating
  Nature* (2006)
Minding Animals: Awareness, Emotions, and Heart (2002)
*The Ten Trusts: What We Must Do to Care for the Animals We
  Love*, with Jane Goodall (2002)
*Strolling with Our Kin: Speaking For and Respecting Voiceless
  Animals* (2000)
Species of Mind: The Philosophy and Biology of Cognitive Ethology,
  with Colin Allen (1997)
Nature's Life Lessons: Everyday Truths from Nature, with Jim
  Carrier (1996)

EDITOR/COEDITOR

*Encyclopedia of Human-Animal Relationships: A Global
  Exploration of Our Connections with Animals*, 4 vols. (2007)
Listening to Cougar, with Cara Blessley Lowe (2007)
Encyclopedia of Animal Behavior (2004)
*The Cognitive Animal: Empirical and Theoretical Perspectives on
  Animal Cognition*, with Colin Allen and Gordon M. Burghardt
  (2002)
The Smile of a Dolphin: Remarkable Accounts of Animal Emotions
  (2000)
*Animal Play: Evolutionary, Comparative, and Ecological
  Perspectives*, with John A. Byers (1998)
Encyclopedia of Animal Rights and Animal Welfare (1998)
Nature's Purposes: Analyses of Function and Design in Biology, with
  Colin Allen and George Lauder (1998)
Readings in Animal Cognition, with Dale Jamieson (1996)

ANIMALS MATTER

A Biologist Explains Why
We Should Treat Animals with
Compassion and Respect

Marc Bekoff

Foreword by Jane Goodall

Shambhala
Boston & London
2007

Shambhala Publications, Inc.
Horticultural Hall
300 Massachusetts Avenue
Boston, Massachusetts 02115
www.shambhala.com

9 8 7 6 5 4 3 2

Printed in the United States of America

♾ This edition is printed on acid-free paper that meets the
American National Standards Institute Z39.48 Standard.

Distributed in the United States by Random House, Inc.,
and in Canada by Random House of Canada Ltd

Interior design and composition: Greta D. Sibley

Library of Congress Cataloging-in-Publication Data
Bekoff, Marc.
Animals matter: a biologist explains why we should treat animals
with compassion and respect /
Marc Bekoff; foreword by Jane Goodall.
p. cm.
Includes bibliographical references and index.
ISBN 978-1-59030-522-5 (alk. paper)
1. Animal welfare. 2. Animal welfare—Moral and ethical aspects.
I. Title.
HV4708.B44 2007
179'.3—dc22
2007012968

For children and young adults everywhere.
May your interactions with our animal kin
be filled with respect, compassion,
spirit, humility, and love.
Keep hope alive even when things seem grim.
Don't let go of your dreams.
There are many better tomorrows.

And for my wonderful parents
who allowed me to pursue
my passions with wild abandon.

Contents

1

The ABC'S of Animal Well-Being and Protection   1

Contents

Contents

Contents

Contents

11

Poisons, Eye Shadow, and Fur   128
Using Animals for Product Testing and Clothing

12

Dissection and Vivisection   145
We Don't Need to Cut Animals to Learn about Life

13

Where to Go from Here?   153
We Are the Key to the Future

Twelve Millennial Mantras   169
by Marc Bekoff and Jane Goodall

Foreword
by Jane Goodall

Whether an individual respects, ignores, or harms different kinds of animals depends, to a large extent, on the kind of environment in which the child grew up, especially the attitudes of family or friends. I was fortunate: when my mother found I'd taken a whole handful of worms to bed with me (I was ten months old), she did not throw them out, but quietly told me they would die without earth, so I toddled with them back into the little bit of garden outside our London apartment. She encouraged my interest in animals. We had a dog and, throughout my childhood, a series of cats and a variety of guinea pigs, hamsters, and so on, which my sister and I were absolutely responsible for—but not allowed to forget. Ever. We were brought up to hate caged things—our canary and subsequently our budgerigar had cage doors left open and flew freely. Our rabbits had the run of the house, the hamster nested in the back of the sofa, and our guinea pigs were regularly taken from their runs and walked, on harnesses, around the streets.

Also, we were encouraged both to explore and interact with the natural world, and to learn about it from the books with which my childhood was surrounded. The most precious of these was a large volume, *The Miracle of Life,* which had been delivered free as a reward for collecting an astronomical number of coupons from packets of some kind of food—cereal probably. That book, with its myriad of illustrations, dealt with topics as diverse as "many tongues for many purposes" and the history of medicine. It was written for adults but it was my passion and helped to shape my respect for life and wonder in nature.

Since those far-off days, before the Second World War, much has changed in the world. There always was abuse of animals, but we are more aware of it today, thanks to the media and the tireless efforts of those who seek to protect creatures of all sorts, from lobsters to chimpanzees, and the environments in which they live. The horror of factory farming is new. The extraordinary explosions of human populations worldwide has caused an ever-increasing hostility between "man" and "beast" as they compete for dwindling resources—and the natural world is losing out. The grim inner-city areas and the poverty that exists even in the most affluent countries increasingly alienate children from nature.

There is a new need for information that will encourage young people to understand the natural world and their relationships to it. A new need to teach children in school about the way their societies treat animals. And a new need to provide our youth with opportunities that foster respect for all life and an empathy with the animal beings with whom we human beings share the planet. This is why I developed the Roots & Shoots program, which enables young people to choose and participate in projects that benefit the environment, animals, and the human community. This program carries two major messages: that every individual matters and can make a difference, every day; and "Only when we understand can we care. Only when we care shall we help. Only if we help will all be saved." We must encourage our young people and empower them to help us save the world that will, so soon, be theirs. There is a vast amount of information about issues of animal abuse and conservation in a vast number of books, magazines, and the children's sections of major conservation and animal welfare organizations. Marc Bekoff has pulled this information together and written about it with clarity and conviction. This is a reference book that can be helpful to students, parents, and teachers alike. It tackles all aspects of our relationships with animals, both in the wild and in the home. It deals with ethical issues about the way we exploit animals, and think about them—not only in relation to ourselves, but as beings in their own right with their own needs, to be celebrated and respected.

When young people have access to good information that enables them to have a good understanding of these issues, their logic is often impeccable. My grandson grew up in Tanzania surrounded by people who look upon fishing as a way of life. At the same time he was always encouraged to respect animals. When he was five years old, he spent a good deal of time with one of our Roots & Shoots volunteers.

One day he asked his father where the fish on his plate came from. Was it killed for him? In that case, please, he did not want to eat any more fish. At the same time, and quite independently, his sister (then three years old) asked similar questions about the chicken served for dinner—with the same result. When I checked with the volunteer, she said she had not advocated vegetarianism—though she is one herself. I too am a vegetarian, though her father is not. But the volunteer told me she had talked a lot about how animals feel—and the children had figured things out for themselves.

If young people know about the terrible cruelty that may result from the pet trade, they will understand why it is a mistake to buy an exotic animal. If they are exposed to what often goes on behind the scenes in seemingly good zoos, they will view the animals there differently. The more they learn, the more they will begin asking questions about issues they were unaware of before.

If knowledge of animals leads to respect and concern for their welfare, the reverse can be true also. Every time a reluctant student is forced to dissect a once-living creature in class, it will be that much easier the next time. There are other ways to learn respect for living forms, to wonder at the amazing way they function—ways that are not destructive of life.

Marc Bekoff encourages young people to think for themselves, to question the status quo. His book will provide parents and teachers with invaluable information about subjects about which they may know little, such as animal intelligence, their capacity to feel pain, their use in pharmaceutical testing, medical experimentation, intensive farming, and training for entertainment. The subjects covered are fairly exhaustive.

Above all, *Animals Matter* will encourage the natural curiosity of young people in their world, foster a sense of wonder and delight, and a corresponding sense of concern. And young people who are kind to and respectful of animals are likely to show more understanding in their relations with other humans as they grow up. I hope this book will be available in all libraries and on the shelves in many homes. It is recommended reading for all the members of our Roots & Shoots program. And this program is growing so fast. Today there are groups in almost 100 countries, and somewhere between 8,000 and 9,000 active groups. The members range from preschoolers through college and university, with a growing number of adult groups as well. These groups are communicating with one another around the world, sharing their projects and their excitement about the changes they are able to make. The Web site (www.rootsandshoots.org) gives a wonderful feeling for the variety of ways in which young people who have access to the facts and are empowered to act are making the world a better place for all living things.

—*Jane Goodall, DBE*
Founder, The Jane Goodall Institute
& UN Messenger of Peace
www.janegoodall.org
www.rootsandshoots.org

Preface

The first edition of this book was published in 2000 under the title *Strolling with Our Kin: Speaking For and Respecting Voiceless Animals* by the American Anti-Vivisection Society and distributed by Lantern Books. It was written for young readers, as a brief and simplified introduction to the many complex ethical issues surrounding the use of animals, especially in scientific research and education, but also in everyday choices concerning preferences such as food, clothing, and entertainment. Many adult readers, including parents, teachers, and others beginning to learn about the importance of animal protection, have also embraced the book as a helpful overview.

Strolling with Our Kin has enjoyed success in German, Italian, Spanish, Japanese, and Chinese editions—a measure of the tremendous worldwide concern over cruelty to animals and a growing global movement to make life better for animals of all kinds. Over the last seven years, it is amazing to see the many new developments in animal rights and animal welfare (both positive and negative), as evidenced by daily news reports from all over the world, ranging from alerts on the suffering of elephants caged in zoos to the first conservation efforts on behalf of Iraqi bird populations, from the horrors of factory farming to a historic move to end primate experiments.

This new edition, under the title *Animals Matter,* has been reedited and updated with some of these new developments. The resources section has been updated, and a glossary and index have been added. I am pleased that the book will continue to awaken readers to the plight of our animal kin and inspire them to take a stand on the animals' behalf.

—*Marc Bekoff*
Boulder, Colorado

Acknowledgments

I thank Katherine Lewis, Dodi Boone, and Stephanie Shain at the AAVS for their detailed and very helpful comments on the manuscript of the first edition of this book (*Strolling with Our Kin*). Sara Goering, Gary Francione, Margaret Wallace, Carron Meaney, Marjorie Bekoff, Barbara Fiedler, Bruce Gottlieb, Marta Turnbull, Bernie Rollin, Dale Jamieson, Colin Allen, Susan Townsend, and Jeff Masson also read an early draft and/or discussed with me many of the issues considered. I also want to thank Kendra Crossen Burroughs for giving this book new life and for a superb editing job.

1

The ABC'S of Animal Well-Being and Protection

The motto of this book is "Always Be Caring and Sharing"—
what I call the ABC'S of animal protection. A compassionate and generous attitude toward all living things will be our
guide as we look at some of the numerous scientific and ethical
issues that we must consider when we discuss relationships
between humans and other animals. (To make things simple, I
will use the word *animal* to refer to nonhuman animal beings,
recognizing of course that humans are animals as well.) It will
become clear that the nature of animal-human encounters—
how animals are viewed and treated—has large and often irreversible impacts on the many different environments in which
we live.

As you read this book, you will discover that there are close
connections among the various kinds of questions we will look
at—such as whether or not animals are as valuable as humans,
whether or not animals have rights, whether or not animals are
conscious, whether or not animals have emotional lives and a
point of view on the situations in which they find themselves,
whether or not animals feel pain and suffer, and whether or not
individual animals count more than entire species. The answers

that are given for such questions greatly influence how we humans view other animals and interact with them. I often begin lectures asking, "Does anyone think that dogs don't experience joy and sadness?" There is never an enthusiastic response to this question, even in scientific gatherings. But when I ask, "Who believes that dogs have feelings?" most hands wave wildly and people smile and nod in agreement, even in scientific venues but often with less passion. And, when someone questions whether dogs experience emotions—the ups and downs of everyday life—I say I'm glad I'm not their dog! The same can be said for many other animals who are routinely used and abused by humans.

Nowadays, more and more people consider these questions to be of great importance. People in all walks of life are asking: Is it right for us to do *anything* we want to animals, just because we are human beings, supposedly the "master" species— just because we *can*? Or should we do everything we can to make sure that the animals we come into contact with are happy, respected, and well cared for? In universities, researchers in many areas—including biology, philosophy, psychology, anthropology, sociology, history, religious studies, and law—are all working together to provide answers for the many and complex questions concerning animal-human interactions. In addition, many people outside of these professions spend a great deal of time and energy trying to make the lives of animals better for the animals themselves. Fortunately, there are many of us who are convinced that the lives of animals are important— that they matter very much—and we try very hard to make animals' lives the best they can be. We believe that humans should never interfere negatively in the lives of animals, especially on purpose. Humans are not the "master" species but one among many species on earth.

Why I am writing this book: The view from within biology

I am a biologist, who deeply cherishes the diverse and wondrous life on this splendid planet. My early scientific training as an undergraduate and a beginning graduate student was grounded in the notion of objectivity—what the philosopher Bernard Rollin calls the "common sense of science." In this approach, science is viewed as a "value-free" activity purely concerned with gathering facts. Of course, science is not value-free—we all come to our lives with a point of view. But it took some time for me to come to this realization, because of the heavy indoctrination and arrogance of my training. Indeed, if science were value-free, my critics would leave me alone.

In supposedly objective science, animals are regarded as *objects* of study, not as *subjects* or experiencers of their own lives. In doing research on or about animals, we were taught to number animals instead of giving them names, in order to discourage us from bonding with them. However, naming and bonding with the animals whom I study is one way for me to respect them. Although some researchers believe that naming animals is a bad idea because named animals will be treated differently than numbered animals—usually less objectively—others believe just the opposite: that naming animals is a *good* idea. As Christopher Manes (1997) observed about many Western cultures, "If the world of our meaningful relationships is measured by the things we call by name, then our universe of meaning is rapidly shrinking. No culture has dispensed personal names as parsimoniously as ours . . . officially limiting personality to humans . . . [and] animals have become increasingly nameless. Some*thing* not some*body*."

Even scientists who know what is going on can sometimes have trouble breaking through their own jargon-garbled "objectivity" in order to tell it like it is. To read their convoluted explanations is to feel as if you have entered the theater of the absurd. Recently I read a report about pain in pigs that concluded: "The observed changes of acoustical parameters during the surgical period can be interpreted as vocal indicators for experienced pain and suffering. We conclude that a careful analysis of the vocal behavior of animals may help to gain a deeper knowledge of pain, stress and discomfort that an animal perceives. The results deliver further facts for a critical re-evaluation of the current practice of non-anaesthetized castration of piglets" (Puppe et al. 2005). This is a roundabout way of saying that castrating young pigs (surgically removing their testicles) without anesthesia—a routine procedure in domestic pig production—hurts. The piglets do not like it, as evidenced by their squeals and attempts to struggle and escape their horrible situation. The researchers conclude that perhaps—just perhaps, mind you—the screams of animals really mean something after all.

Jane Goodall (1999), the world-famous expert on chimpanzee behavior and tireless crusader for generating human respect for animal lives, notes that early in her career she learned that naming animals and describing their personalities was taboo in science, but because she had not been to university she did not know this. She "thought it was silly and paid no attention." Dr. Goodall opposed reductionistic, mechanistic science early in her career, as she does now, and her bold efforts have had much influence on developing scientists' views of animals as thinking and feeling beings.

The eyes of a cat influenced my development as a scientist. I was working on a research project for my doctoral degree in which we were supposed to kill the cats we were studying. However, when I went to get Speedo, a very intelligent cat who

I'd secretly named (secretly, because we weren't supposed to name our "subjects"), his fearlessness disappeared as if he knew that this was his last journey. As I picked him up, he looked at me and seemed to ask, "Why me?" Tears came to my eyes. He wouldn't break his piercing stare. Though I followed through with what I was required to do and killed him, it broke my heart to do so. To this day I remember his unwavering eyes— they told the whole story of the interminable pain and indignity he had endured. Other students in the program tried to reassure me that it was all worth it, but I never recovered from that experience.

As a scientist, I have been lucky to have studied social behavior in coyotes in the Grand Teton National Park in Jackson, Wyoming; the development of behavior in Adélie penguins in Antarctica near the South Pole; and social behavior in various birds living near my home in the Rocky Mountains of Colorado. I have learned a lot about these amazing animals and many others. I am very concerned about what humans are doing to other animals and to the planet in general. Some of my views may make it seem as if I want to stop *all* animal research, including my own, and the human use of all animals everywhere, but this is not so. I am just not very happy with what is happening to the wonderful animals with whom I am privileged to live and share the earth. Are you?

In this short book I will discuss some broad and interrelated topics and raise numerous questions about how animals and humans interact—and about the ways animals are used for mostly human benefit. Each topic makes a number of points. All topics are related to the main issue: *the choices people make when we interact with other animals with whom we are privileged to share the planet.*

I have also compiled a list of resources in the back of the book, to help readers learn more about these and other topics, because some of the questions that need to be considered are difficult and it is helpful to see what others have to say about them. There is always something to be learned from others' views.

I hope this book will appeal to people of all ages and in different cultures, because the issues I discuss and the questions I pose have few if any boundaries with respect to age, culture, and time. I am also hoping that this primer will serve to generate many more questions than those I raise, and that perhaps some people will be able to read it together and discuss questions as they arise. Brothers and sisters can read it to one another, and parents, teachers, and other adults can read it along with children. Young children are very interested in most animals. Their initial contacts usually are friendly and show that they do not recognize many large differences between themselves and other animals. When my nephew, Aaron, was two years old, he knelt, went nose-to-nose with a worm, and said, "Hello." At seventeen, Aaron still is naturally attracted to animals.

Much of what children come to believe about and feel for animals is learned and influenced by early environments. Older children and adults can play major roles in developing children's attitudes that have long-lasting effects. Jane Goodall's foreword says this all very nicely.

Moderation and consistency in using animals

Most people take a moderate position on animal use by humans. They accept some uses of animals but not all. They feel all right about the use of some animals rather than others. For these people, not all animals are equal. They often find it difficult to be consistent and objective. Maybe it would be acceptable to use chimpanzees to save their own mother's or child's life, but not the life of someone else's mother or child. Perhaps it is fine to confine a fish to an aquarium or a bird to a cage, but not a gorilla to a zoo. As Lisa Mighetto (1991) emphasizes, "Those who complain of the 'inconsistencies' of animal lovers understand neither the complexity of attitudes nor how rapidly they have developed." Even with our inconsistencies and contradictions when dealing with the difficult issues centering on animal protection, we have come a long way in dealing with many, but not all, of the problems. But we should not be complacent, for there still are far too many animals suffering at the hands of humans, and much work still needs to be done. I am not trying to criticize these people, for the issues are very difficult. But some degree of consistency and perhaps *strong* guidelines are necessary to guide us so that we can lessen the pain and suffering that humans cause to other animals every second of every day.

Why all the concern about how animals are treated by humans? Why do some people spend a large portion of their lives studying animal-human interactions rather than playing games, going on vacations, or trying to learn about other interesting aspects of the wondrous world in which we all live? When many people sit back and look around at the world, they realize that they are too far removed from the other animals—and even too far removed from plants, rocks, and streams—with whom they share the planet Earth. This distance has made the world a mess—with lethal pollution, too many cars, too much disease, too much stress, too many people, and too many abused animals whose lives have been ruined. Many people are coming to realize that they are *a part* of the rest of nature and not *apart* from it. *No one is outside nature.* These people want to do something for all beings with whom they share the precious and limited resources on earth. What could be a better place to start than with the other animals—our kin—with whom we share our one and only wondrous but increasingly fragile planet.

Why you *are so important*

Why are you so important? What difference can you make? Why should you care about other animals and the environment? It is very easy to answer this question. We all live on this planet, and we all inherit the earth that others leave behind. By thinking about these issues, it is likely that you will become more closely attached to the other living organisms and inanimate objects around you. Animals count, trees count, and rocks count. But all too often we live as if future generations do not count. What will happen if people in the future inherit the messes we leave? We need to share our lessons with one another, for what people learn will influence how they think and act.

It is important to encourage everyone to explore the ways animals live, important for all of us to want animals' lives to be the best they can, and important for you to ask questions about how humans treat other animals. It is important for children to know that hamburgers were once cows, that the bacon on a bacon, lettuce, and tomato sandwich was once a pig, and that cows, pigs, chickens, and fish are social animals and have families just like humans. Both the cow and the pig were once someone's child, brother, or sister. They had lives that were ended so that people could eat them. They were removed from their mothers or families, housed in horrible conditions, shipped to commercial food-processing plants, and killed, suffering all the way. While this description sounds awful, and it could be "cleaned up" and colored by using other words to make it less offensive, this really is what happens to cows, pigs, and other animals who become human meals. If we do not tell it like it is, important messages are lost.

Teaching and practicing tolerance unquestionably are good habits to incorporate into all of our lives. We need to develop and to *live* an ethic of caring and sharing so that all animals are respected for the individuals they are. Perhaps the best way to state it is that we need to recognize that we are privileged to live on such a wonderfully diverse planet that is full of incredible and bountiful beauty. In order that our children, our children's children, and their children in turn can fully enjoy the beauty and grandeur that nature offers, everyone must give very serious attention to how animals are viewed and treated. *We are so lucky to have so many other animals as our friends.*

Habitat loss and planetary biodiversity

Globally and locally, within small communities, there is much interest in the many and difficult questions concerning how humans interact with and treat animals. Of course, as we will see, global and local issues are closely related to one another. How and why humans and animals interact in nature, in industry, in zoos, wildlife theme parks, and aquariums, and in research laboratories are very important and controversial topics all over the world.

Globally, populations of humans are growing rapidly, and many populations of wild animals and plants continue to lose their battle with humans. Global biodiversity—the number of different species that inhabit our planet—is rapidly, and perhaps irreversibly, dwindling. In August 1998 a front-page story in the *New York Times* declared: "It Is Kenya's Farmers vs.

Wildlife, and the Animals Are Losing." Indeed, 58% of the animals in Kenya's Tsavo region, about 106,000 large mammals, vanished between 1973 and 1993. Nowadays, scientists claim that wildlife extinction rates are soaring, and the die-off threatens our planet's biodiversity, which sustains farming, forestry, and oceans. When 1,200 scientists met at an international conference sponsored by the government of France in 2005, they issued a statement at the end of the five-day event. It said in part, "Biodiversity is being irreversibly destroyed by human activities at an unprecedented rate . . . [demanding] urgent and significant action."[1]

Clearly, problems like Kenya's concerning farming, tourism, human interests and needs, and the fate of wild animals are global issues. They demand close attention now because of the enormous uncontrolled growth in the number of humans all over the planet, the decline of habitat where animals can live (in Kenya it is estimated that wild lands are disappearing at a rate of 2% a year), and the rampant use of animals to meet human needs and desires.

On the global level, many researchers think that the main problem is fairly simple—there are too many people and not enough land for them. Indeed, habitat loss is considered by most conservation biologists to be the biggest threat to animal and plant life. Uncontrolled habitat loss means there will be a loss in global biodiversity. Even if humans want to reintroduce species to the wild or relocate them to suitable habitats where they would be able to thrive and survive, such places will not be available, because while the animals are not there, humans continue to develop the area and make it impossible to place them there at a later time.

---

1. http://news.minnesota.publicradio.org/features/2005/01/31_olsond _biodiversity.

Animal use: The numbers speak for themselves

In addition to global issues concerning biodiversity, there are also local concerns centered on individual animals rather than on entire ecosystems, populations, or species. Because there are so many people, the demand for animal products and for dealing with human medical needs and food requirements is rising astronomically.

Let's first consider the number of animals who are used for food under rampantly inhumane conditions in factory farming and commercial food plants. Animals used for human meals far outnumber individual animals used for other purposes. People usually tell me that they had no idea that the numbers were so high. I'm personally proud that the people who prepared the index for my book *Minding Animals* became vegetarians after they saw the numbers, so let's see what the numbers say. In the United States alone, some 26.8 billion (26,843,600,000, to be exact) animals were killed for food in 1998. These figures break down to 73,424,657 animals per day, 3,059,361 animals per hour, 50,989 animals per minute, and 850 animals per second slaughtered for food in the United States. As many as 12% of chickens and 14% of pigs die of stress, injury, or diseases because of the appalling conditions of today's factory farms. Ingrid Newkirk, founder of People for the Ethical Treatment of Animals (PETA), notes that animals are also used in commercial pet food, where they find themselves in containers called "4-D bins." The D's stand for the Dead, Dying, Diseased, and Disabled individuals who are eaten by our companion animals. Slaughterhouses are truly "weapons of mass destruction."

What about the use of animals in laboratory research? According to Larry Carbone (2004), about 690,800 guinea pigs, rabbits, and hamsters were used in American laboratories in

11

2001, along with 70,000 dogs, 49,400 primates, 22,800 cats, 161,700 farm animals (they get no break), and 80 million mice and rats. While these numbers are small compared with the commercial food industry, in which billions of animals suffer horrifically and interminably, it's sickening to think about the lives that laboratory animals live and to know what they must be feeling in their cages. Recent studies demonstrate that mice feel empathy for other mice who are in pain, so not only do they suffer from the way in which they themselves are treated, but they also feel the pain of other mice. In 2006, researchers discovered that mice who watch their peers in pain are more sensitive to it themselves and that an injected mouse writhed more if its partner was also writhing. Mice used visual cues to generate the empathic response, although they typically use odor in many of their social encounters. In response to this recent discovery, it was suggested by one researcher that an opaque barrier be used to separate mice so that they can't know what's happening to another mouse, because mice who observe each other during experiments may be "contaminating" the data.

The scientific community has created a set of professional standards that is supposed to guide scientists in how to develop and conduct their research so as to preserve animal welfare as much as possible, and in theory animals used in research in the United States are protected by the federal Animal Welfare Act. But these safeguards have so far been inadequate. Only about 1% of animals used in research in the United States are protected by this legislation, and the legislation is sometimes amended in nonsensical ways to accommodate the "needs" of researchers. For instance, here is a quote from the *Federal Register* 69, no. 108, June 4, 2004: "We are amending the Animal Welfare Act (AWA) regulations to reflect an amendment to the Act's definition of the term *animal*. The

Farm Security and Rural Investment Act of 2002 amended the definition of *animal* to specifically exclude birds, rats of the genus *Rattus,* and mice of the genus *Mus,* bred for use in research."

It may surprise you to hear that birds, rats, and mice are not considered animals, but that's the sort of logic that epitomizes federal legislators: since researchers are not "allowed" to abuse animals, the definition of "animal" is simply revised until it only refers to creatures researchers don't need.

After this scientific study of empathy in mice appeared, I received numerous stories about empathy in a wide variety of animals, including rodents. People who live with animals weren't surprised by the findings. CeAnn Lambert, who runs the Indiana Coyote Rescue Center, told that me that one hot summer morning she saw two baby mice in a deep sink in her garage. They were trying to get out of the sink but couldn't get up the steep, slick sides. One of the mice seemed to be less exhausted than the other. CeAnn put some water in a lid and placed it in the sink, and immediately the more lively baby went over to get a drink. On the way to the water, the mouse found a piece of food and picked it up and took it over to its littermate. The weak mouse tried to take a bite of the food while the other kept moving the food slowly toward the water. Finally, the weaker mouse got a drink. Both gained some strength and climbed out using a board that CeAnn placed in the sink.

Government workers also kill numerous animals. For example, some people who work for the Bureau of Land Management and the U.S. Fish and Wildlife Service "recreationally shoot" and kill prairie dogs in order to control populations of these beautiful rodents. The Animal Damage Control (ADC) unit (now called Wildlife Services) of the U.S. Department of Agriculture is responsible for cruelly and indiscriminately killing hundreds of thousands animals—"varmints" or "pests" as officials call them—including coyotes (about 76,000 in 2004), foxes (about 4,300), and mountain lions (359) in the name of control and management.[2] Wildlife Services killed about 83,000 mammalian predators in 2004. However, only about 1% of livestock losses are due to predators, and 99% are due to disease, exposure to bad weather, illness, starvation, dehydration, and deaths at birth. The ADC has also been responsible for reducing the populations of at least eleven endangered species.[3]

Numerous animals are subject to genetic engineering, bred by scientists to develop heart failure, for example, at an early age, for the purposes of research. Although some animals are genetically engineered to develop resistance to disease, this is done for the benefit of people, not for the animals themselves, and the degree of suffering and death of "designer animals" makes the practice of genetic tampering controversial. Genetically altered food—dubbed "frankenfood" by critics also is becoming very widespread.[4] Furthermore, bovine growth hormone (rBGH) is being used to increase milk production by cows, despite its demonstrated risks to the health of cattle (increased udder infections and foot diseases) and humans (possible increased risk of breast cancer). The Humane Farming Association is leading a national campaign to protect consumers from the dangers of antibiotics, hormones, and other chemicals used on factory farms, and to protect farm animals from being abused for profit. Bernard Rollin has written about

---

2. www.goagro.org/WS04Kill.pdf.
3. For a summary see www.aphis.usda.gov/ws/tables/TABLE%2010 Killed,%20FY%202004.pdf.
4. See www.organicconsumers.org, www.biointegrity.org, and www.safe-food.org.

these issues in his book *The Frankenstein Syndrome* (1995), as has Michael W. Fox in *Beyond Evolution* (1999). We also need to be deeply concerned about the well-being of the millions of companion animals ("pets"). A survey by the American Veterinary Medical Association showed that in 2001 there were about 61,572,000 dogs, 70,796,000 cats, and 10,105,000 birds kept in homes in the United States. There were also about 5,107,000 companion horses. Millions of exotic animals also are kept as companions, including about 50 million fish (though it is very difficult to estimate the number of fish kept in homes), 1 million ferrets, 5 million rabbits, 630,000 gerbils, and 1 million turtles.[5]

A lot of money is spent on companion animals. One study found that money spent on pets in the United States will have more than doubled from $17 billion in 1994 to about $35.9 billion for 2005. In 2004, U.S. pet owners spent $34.4 billion on their pets, making the pet industry larger than the toy industry, in which about $20 billion was spent. According to this study, in 2004, dog owners spent an average $211 on routine veterinary visits, and cat owners spent $179.[6]

Far too many companion animals are permitted to reproduce, resulting in an overpopulation of unwanted individuals. Many are ignored or abused when they become burdensome to their human companions. Programs directly concerned with the well-being and fate of companion animals include First Strike, run by the Humane Society of the United States, devoted to raising awareness about the relationship between cruelty to animals and human violence. It has been found that violence toward pets is often a predictor of abuse of family members in the same

5. www.avma.org/membshp/marketstats/comp_exotic.asp.
6. See www.avma.org/onlnews/javma/jul05/050701k.asp.

home. First Strike works to prevent such cruelty and domestic abuse and to promote anti-cruelty legislation.

The more-than-human world

When human populations show explosive growth, it is other animals that suffer—entire ecosystems, species, populations, and individuals. The end result is clear: animals lose when human interests come into conflict with animal interests.

The problems we face in the area of animal-human interactions raise numerous questions, many of which I consider below. For example, how should humans treat animals? There is much interest in whether or not humans *should* treat animals in particular ways. Do we *have* to treat animals in certain ways? Are there right and wrong ways for humans to treat animals? Can we do whatever we want to animals? Do we need to respect animals' *rights*? Do animals even have rights? And if animals have rights, what exactly *are* those rights? People interested in issues of animal-human relationships are concerned with the *ethics* of these interactions.

Ethics is a branch of philosophy concerned with issues of rightness or fairness and how we should behave toward one another. However, it is important to emphasize that for questions about the treatment of animals, there are often no clear-cut "right" and "wrong" answers. Instead, there are "better" and "worse" answers. Open discussion of all sides will help us make progress. We can't dismiss anyone's point of view by pretending that it does not exist. Ignoring conflicts will not make them disappear. How we relate to animals is closely related to how we relate to ourselves and to other humans. We are all in this life together, and if we are not part of the solution, most likely we are part of the problem.

David Abram (1996), a philosopher and storyteller, reminds us that we live in a "more-than-human world." Native Americans are proud to proclaim that "animals are all our relations." These are important messages because they stress the close, intimate, and reciprocal relationships that exist between animals and humans. Animals are our kin. It is important to realize how much animals do for us. They teach us about trust and respect. Animals also teach us about responsibility. In return, we need to make sure that all animals have every opportunity to be happy and content. Compassion and respect are the least that we can give back to them.

It is also important to remember that when humans choose to *use* animals, the animals invariably have no say in these decisions. They cannot give their consent. Animals depend on our goodwill and mercy. They depend on humans to have their best interests in mind.

Speaking for voiceless animals

Humans are constantly making decisions for numerous animals. *We are their voices.* However, we also know that animals tell us how they are feeling using many types of vocalizations— ranging from purring by cats to show contentment to squealing by young unanesthetized pigs when their teeth are ground down on a grindstone or their tail is cut off with a pair of scissors. But when we speak for them, in order for there to be balance, we need to be sure that we are taking into account their best interests. As Jane Goodall (1990) has said: "The least I can do is to speak out for the hundreds of chimpanzees who, right now, sit hunched, miserable and without hope, staring out with dead eyes from the metal prisons. They cannot speak for themselves." My companion dog Jethro cannot tell me in any human language whether it is all right for me to feed or walk him now, nor can laboratory rats tell me that they agree to be used in an experiment in which they will feel pain and suffer, and perhaps be killed. When scientists use chimpanzees for behavioral or medical research, they do not ask them if they agree to be kept in a small cage alone, be injected with a virus, have blood drawn, and then perhaps be "sacrificed"—killed—so that the psychological and physiological effects of the experiment can be studied in more detail.

Because of our dominant position in the world, because we can freely speak and express our feelings about animals, who do not have much say in the matter, it might *seem* as if animals exist for humans to use in any way we choose. However, ethical values tell us that animals should not be viewed as property, as resources, or as disposable machines who exist for human consumption, treated like bicycles or backpacks. Just because we *can* exercise power doesn't mean we *have* to do it; we have a choice. And just because certain activities *seem* to have worked in the past does not mean that they truly have worked. For example, in the past, most people believed that in order to make human life better, we had to perform experimental research on animals, even if that meant disrupting their lives and bodies in violent ways. Eating the flesh of animals was also believed to be indispensable to human health. Today we know that both of these practices—invasive experimentation and meat eating—are not necessary to a good life for humans, and people increasingly consider them to be cruel and unethical. Although we cannot undo all the mistakes people have made with animals, there is still time—perhaps not a lot of time—to make changes that will help both us and other animals to have better lives.

Unfortunately, modern people are largely detached from nature and the outdoors in general. A recent survey showed that most people spend more than 95% of their lives indoors.

One result of this alienation from nature is that it causes us to lose our feeling of kinship with animals and encourages us to treat them like mere objects, to do with whatever we want. Let us remember that animals are not mere resources for human consumption. They are splendid beings in their own right, who have evolved alongside us as co-inheritors of all the beauty and abundance of life on this planet.

I hope that this book promotes open discussion about the way we treat animals. Open discussion, in which we listen to everyone's point of view, can make us better people and also can make the world a better place to live in. We will therefore look at some opposing viewpoints in this book, because it can be useful to adopt the position opposite to the one that you agree with and try to defend it. You then can imagine what your opponents are thinking and how they developed their own thoughts and feelings about animal-human interactions.

Minding animals: A personal story

A good place to begin is with a few anecdotes about my own experiences with animals. Growing up, I did not have the company of many animals. From time to time there were some goldfish and little painted turtles with whom to share my life. I loved them and watched them do what they do.

When I was very young, my parents tell me, I always "minded" animals. "Minding animals" means that I cared for them and simply assumed that they had very active brains. I also knew that they had minds! I never doubted that they were very smart. I always asked, "What do you think they're thinking? What's on their minds? What do you think they're feeling?" I never doubted that animals had minds and were just like us in many ways.

Of course, later I came to realize that animals have their own points of view, but by using human terms to describe animal emotions and behavior—they are happy, sad, angry, jealous—it made it easier to tell myself and others what might be happening in their heads. It also struck me as odd that many people who thought that animals could have *negative* emotions—that they could be angry, mean, or depressed and treated with antidepressants—were uncomfortable when people ascribed *positive* emotions to animals—that they could be happy and enjoy life.

Not until I was twenty-six years old did I have the wonderful experience of sharing my life with a companion dog. Moses was a large white malamute who blessed my life for only a short period of time. He was a bundle of joy who made me realize how much I had missed as a kid. Because I was in graduate school studying animal behavior, it was natural to include Moses in my circle of dearest friends. When he was two and a half years old, he died while being treated for a hangnail. Really, a simple hangnail. The veterinarian gave him a mild sedative, and Moses had an allergic reaction to it and died suddenly. I was devastated. How could this happen? How could I cope with his absence? It was the first time in a long while that I had experienced such a great loss, and it made me even more determined to live with and to study animals for the rest of my life. I wanted to learn more about how they perceive their own lives, how and why animals come to mean so much to so many people, and what I could do to make their lives better for *them*, regardless of what I or other humans wanted or needed.

Missing Mom: Candid coyotes

Here is a story that always creeps into my mind when I think about animal tales that show how "minding animals" can help us understand their lives. Years after this incident happened, it still rings clearly in my memory.

My students and I studied coyotes for seven years around Blacktail Butte, in the Grand Teton National Park, south of Jackson, Wyoming. A female whom we called "Mom" was a mother and a wife from the beginning of the study until late 1980 when she began leaving her family for short forays. She would just take off and disappear for a few hours and then return to the pack as if nothing had happened. I wondered if her family missed her when she wandered about. It sure seemed that they did. When Mom left for forays that lasted for longer and longer periods of time, often a day or two, some pack members would look at her curiously before she left—they would cock their head to the side and squint and furrow their brows as if they were asking, "Where are you going now?" Some of her children would even follow her for a while. When Mom returned, they would greet her effusively by whining loudly, licking her muzzle, wagging their tails like windmills, and rolling over in front of her in glee. "Mom's back!"

One day Mom left the pack and never again returned. The pack waited impatiently for days and days. Some coyotes paced nervously about like expectant parents, while others went off on short trips, only to return alone. They traveled in the direction she had gone, sniffed in places she might have visited, and howled as if calling her home. For more than a week, some spark seemed to be gone. Her family missed her. I think the coyotes would have cried if they could have.

After a while, life returned to normal on Blacktail Butte: sleep, eat, play a little, hunt, defend the territory, rest, and travel. A new and unfamiliar female joined the pack, was accepted by all the coyotes, formed a partnership with the breeding dominant male, and eventually gave birth to eight babies. Now *she* was mom and wife. But every now and again it seemed that some of the pack members still missed the original Mom—maybe she was lost; maybe she would return if we went to look for her. The coyotes would sit up, look around, raise their noses to the wind, head off on short trips in the direction that Mom last went, and return weary without her. It took about three or four months until these searches ended. Pack members still seemed to miss Mom, but it was time for them to move on.

It was clear to me and my students that coyotes, like many other animals, have deep and complicated feelings. I'll never forget this lesson in animal emotions that Mom and her family taught me.

A "rabbit punch" changes my life

Here is another story of some events that changed my life. One afternoon, during a graduate course in physiology, one of my professors strutted into class sporting a wide grin while carrying a live rabbit and calmly announced that he was going to kill a rabbit for us to use in a later experiment, by using a method named after the rabbit himself, namely a "rabbit punch." He killed the rabbit in front of the class by breaking his neck by chopping him with the side of his hand. I was astonished and sickened by the entire spectacle. I refused to partake in the laboratory exercise and also decided that the graduate program in which I was enrolled was not for me. I began to think seriously about alternatives. I enjoyed science and continue to enjoy doing scientific research, but I imagined that there were other ways of doing science that incorporated respect for animals and allowed individuals to conduct science according to their own ethical values instead of being forced to follow cruel conventions of the field. I went on to another graduate program, but dropped out because I did not want to kill dogs in physiology laboratories or cats in a research project. (I later learned that the famous biologist Charles Darwin also dropped out of medical school after one year, quite possibly because of his repulsion at experiments on dogs. In his 1871 book *The Descent of Man*, Darwin wrote about someone who experimented on dogs: "...this man, unless he had a heart of stone, must have felt remorse to the last hour of his death.") Finally, I found a graduate program in which I could watch animals and record what they did, without having to kill them to learn about their exciting and unique lives.

It is all right to care about animals

Now, the reason I am telling you some of my personal stories is not to preach that my approach to science is the only right one. Rather, it is to make a few points. First, while having contact with animals early in life might be important for developing empathy and feelings for them, it is not necessary to have been raised alongside animals. Also, it is possible for people to change their views on animals. I have changed my mind about what I can and cannot do to animals, and so have a number of my colleagues.

Some researchers do not like to form close bonds with the animals they study because they think it influences their research, which is supposed to be objective. However, Konrad Lorenz—the famous Nobel Prize–winning ethologist, or specialist in animal behavior—believed that it is all right for researchers to bond with the animals they study, that in fact we should *love* the animals we study. Respecting and forming bonds with the animals you study might make you view them very differently than if you considered them to be mere objects. When we love animals instead of just treating them like "things," we begin to appreciate them for who they are in their own worlds, and to view them as *subjects* of a life and not mere objects. Such an attitude can only make science better and more reliable. Why? Because when we respect each animal's point of view, we will stop thinking of animals exclusively from our own points of view and will start to truly understand theirs. As we come to understand how they are and how they sense their world, we will appreciate them and respect them more. And increased appreciation and respect will then mean that we will exert greater efforts to make their lives better because they are living beings, not because they can serve us in one way or another. Although other animals may be *different* from us, this does not make them *less* than us.

Animals have their own lives and their own points of view, and it is important to recognize this. Maybe it is easier to harm animals if we distance ourselves from them—we may think that since they are so different from us that it is okay for us to harm them. But this only makes matters worse, in the end, for us humans. People who do this get so removed from the world around them they cannot appreciate its remarkable beauty and splendor.

It is all right to care about animals. Caring about animals makes us more humane and more human, for we know when we are choosing cruelty over compassion. When we recognize the beauty and value of each and every life, I believe, the world will become a better place, and that better science will result. A compassionate view of the world on the part of humans will make the world a happier place for all of its residents. We are animals' guardians and spokespersons, and we owe them unconditional compassion, respect, and support—just as we do with our fellow human beings. We may have control and "dominion" over other animals, but this does not mean that we have the right to exploit and dominate them. Most importantly, each and every one of us makes a difference.

Some guiding principles

My views on animal minds, animal rights, and doing science with animals have been strongly influenced by the animals' unselfish sharing of their lives with me. I consider myself lucky and privileged to have been able to have made the intimate acquaintance of many different animals, to be touched by who they are as both individuals and members of diverse species. I am sure that in some instances they were watching, smelling, hearing, and studying me as closely as I was observing them. People are often not aware that they are interfering in the lives of the animals in whom they are interested. The following guiding principles for interactions with animals thus stress that it is a *privilege* to share our lives with other animals; we should respect their interests and lives at all times, and give serious attention to the animals' own views of the world.

1. Take seriously the animals' own points of view.
2. Give priority to respect, compassion, and admiration for other animals.
3. When uncertain about whether animals are feeling pain or suffering, assume that they are and act accordingly.
4. Recognize that almost all of the methods used to study animals, even in the wild, are intrusions on their lives, and step into their lives as lightly as possible, if at all.
5. Focus on the importance of individuals, and the diversity of the lives of individual animals in the worlds

within which they live, rather than on species or ecosystems.

6. Appreciate individual variations in behavior and temperament: not all coyotes are the same.
7. Use compassion and empathy when doing scientific research.

Although I have always been concerned with animal protection, I have not always applied the highest standards of conduct to my own research. When I studied predatory behavior in infant coyotes in the mid-1970s, I provided mice and chickens as bait. The coyotes were allowed to chase and kill the mice and chickens, who could not escape. I regret this type of research, and I apologize to the animals that I allowed to be killed. I never again engaged in this kind of research.

Questions to ponder deeply

Now, what are some questions that must be considered when talking about how humans and animals get along? Why should we care about other animals? First, I will list some questions. You will see that many of the questions are related to one another and that we cannot discuss one without discussing others.

Let me stress once again that there are no "right" and "wrong" answers for many, but not for all, of these questions. People who disagree with one another cannot always be called "good" or "bad." There are shades of grey—but perhaps some of the grey areas will become more black or white as they are discussed openly. What is needed now is for each of us to sit down and think about these and other questions in a way that helps make animals' lives become better in the future.

- Why might some people think that is all right to kill dogs rather than other people in biomedical research?
- Why do some people feel more comfortable killing ants rather than dogs?
- Do some animals feel pain, experience anxiety, and suffer, but not others?
- Are some animals conscious?
- Do animals feel emotions?
- Are some animals smart and not others?
- Do some animals have rights and not others?
- Are some species more valuable or more important than others?
- Should endangered animals such as wolves be reintroduced to places where they originally lived?
- Should we be more concerned with species and their survival than with individuals and their well-being?
- Should animals be kept in captivity, in zoos, wildlife theme parks, and aquariums?
- Should we interfere in the lives of animals? For example, should we interfere in fights in which an individual could get hurt? Should we feed starving wildlife? Should we give first-aid when wild animals are hurt? Should we rescue animals from oil spills? Should we inoculate wild animals to protect them from diseases such as rabies?
- Why do some humans eat animals?
- Why do some humans use animals for research?
- Why do many people feel more comfortable using dogs for research rather than experimenting on humans?
- Should animals be used to test cosmetics or foods?
- Should domesticated animals such as dogs and cats be treated differently than their wild relatives, such as wolves and lions?

- Do we need to cut up animals—dissect them—to learn about them or ourselves?
- What types of non-animal alternatives are available for product testing, dissection, and vivisection?
- What kinds of actions are needed to make life better for animals in the future?"

When people tell me that they love animals and then go on to abuse them, I tell them that I'm glad they don't love me. I often ask researchers who conduct invasive work with animals or people who slaughter animals on factory farms, "Would you do it to your dog?" Some are startled to hear this question. If someone won't do something to their dog that they do daily to other dogs or to mice, rats, cats, monkeys, pigs, cows, elephants, or chimpanzees, we need to know why. There's no doubt whatsoever that, when it comes to what we may and may not do to other animals, it's their emotions that should inform our discussions and our actions on their behalf.

Animals have feelings

We all make choices, and the reasons why certain choices are made need to be carefully analyzed and discussed. Some people justify their cruel treatment of animals by saying that animals are cruel to one another, so why can't we be cruel to animals? We will see later on that this is a bad argument and simply not true. It's not a dog-eat-dog world; indeed, dogs do not eat other dogs. Rather, we know that many animals show compassion and empathy toward one another and that they truly care about how their friends are feeling.

While I was watching a group of wild elephants living in the Samburu Reserve in northern Kenya, I noted that one of them,

Babyl, walked very slowly. I learned that she was crippled and that she couldn't travel as fast as the rest of the herd. However, the elephants in Babyl's group didn't leave her behind when they traveled. When I asked the elephant expert Iain Douglas-Hamilton about this, he replied that these elephants always waited for Babyl, and they'd been doing so for years. They'd walk for a while, then stop and look around to see where Babyl was. Depending on how she was doing, they'd either wait or proceed. Iain said the matriarch even fed her on occasion. Why did the other elephants in the herd act this way? Babyl could do little for them, so there was no reason or practical gain for helping her. The obvious explanation is that the other elephants cared for Babyl, and so they adjusted their behavior to allow her to remain with the group. Friendship and empathy go a long way.

Joyce Poole, who has studied African elephants for decades, was told a story about a teenage female who was suffering from a withered leg on which she could put no weight. When a young male from another group began attacking the injured female, a large adult female chased the attacking male, returned to the young female, and touched her crippled leg with her trunk. Poole is certain that the adult female was showing empathy and sympathy.

Bears also display empathy. While I was in Homer, Alaska, I read about two grizzly bear cubs who stuck together after they were orphaned when their mother was shot near the Russian River. The female cub remained with her wounded sibling, who limped and swam very slowly, allowing her brother to eat fish she hauled ashore. An observer noted, "She came out and got a fish, and pulled it back, and then she let the other one eat." The young female obviously cared for her brother, and her support was crucial for his survival.

Animals often support one another and we must support

them too. Their lives must be taken seriously, and it is not enough to argue that the ends justify the means—that human benefits justify our uses and treatment of animals. Often what we claim is "good welfare" is not "good enough." Our emotions are the gifts of our ancestors, our animal kin. We have feelings and so do other animals. We must never forget this.

2

Animals in a Human World

Human and nonhuman primates: How close are we?

Although there are numerous differences between humans and other animals, in many important ways "we" (humans) are very much one of "them" (animals), and "they" are very much one of "us." For example, researchers have compared proteins on the surface of human and chimpanzee cells. Out of nine amino acid chains studied (amino acids are the building blocks of proteins), there are only five (0.4%) differences out of a total of 1,271 amino acid positions. This means we are 99.6% chimpanzee, and vice versa. Also, although it has been commonly reported that humans and chimpanzees share between 98% and 99% of their genes, more recent research shows that the difference between humans and chimpanzees might be about 6%. Still, we are very much chimpanzee and chimpanzees are very much human.[1] Gorillas are about 2.3% different from

---

1. www.sciam.com/article.efm?articleID=9D0DAC2B-E7F2-99DF-3 AA795436FEF8039.

both humans and chimpanzees, and orangutans are about 3.6% different from both humans and chimpanzees.

Despite the close kinship between humans and the great apes—chimpanzees, bonobos, gorillas, and orangutans—when we cross paths with these other animals, the animals often lose. Chimpanzees are used in much research that causes them pain and suffering. They are strapped to chairs and unable to move, subjected to radiation that makes them violently ill and sometimes kills them, shocked in situations from which they cannot escape, and injected with infections that sicken and kill them. They are also used to study diseases, such as AIDS, which means they are deliberately infected with an illness that they otherwise would not naturally contract in the wild. When they are used in these sorts of experiments, they are often housed alone in horribly small cages and suffer severe emotional stress and depression as well as physical trauma including severe weight loss and self-mutilation.

Around the world, movements such as the Great Ape Project have been launched to improve the lives of these magnificent animals and to eliminate their use altogether. Since 1999, New Zealand (1999), the Netherlands (2002), Sweden (2003), and Austria (2006) have banned chimpanzee research, and in 1997 Great Britain placed a ban on licenses for chimpanzee research.[2] Furthermore, all of the countries making up the European Union (EU) have signed the Treaty of Amsterdam, which came into effect on May 1, 1999. This treaty recognizes animals as sentient beings capable of feeling fear and pain, and of enjoying themselves when well treated. When formulating and implementing community policies on agriculture, transport,

---

2. www.releasechimps.org/mission/end-chimpanzee-research/country -bans.

research, and internal trade, the EU must now "pay full regard to the welfare requirements of animals."[3]

Retirement homes

What happens to the animals when researchers are finished with their research? Chimpanzees and other animals are often disposed of when no longer useful. They are "sacrificed" or "euthanized," which means they are killed, or they languish in cages year in and year out. But now there are many people who do not want these animals' lives to end or be wasted just because they are no longer useful to humans. They want to build retirement homes for chimpanzees and other animals whose research careers are over so that these animals have the best lives possible and die a natural death. They want to rehabilitate these individuals whose lives have been damaged psychologically and physically.

One of the most visible cases concerning the fate of research animals centered on the chimpanzees who were used in the United States space program, the "Air Force chimpanzees." While some people want to continue to use these animals in biomedical research because they are no longer needed for space research—simply move them from one cage to another—others want them to be retired in comfort for the remainder of their lives. After all, they did what they were told to do, and endured much pain and suffering during space research. Following a TV show, "Dateline," on which chimpanzee retirement homes were discussed, 98% of the people who responded to a survey favored the use of retirement homes for these animals.

---

3. www.awionline.org/newsletters/aw48-3.html.

One of the biggest businesses that opposed retirement homes was the Coulston Foundation, in Alamogordo, New Mexico. Concerning chimpanzees, their founder, Frederick Coulston, once said: "Why let them retire? I won't retire. Most people I know, even if they retire from a good job, continue to do something good. You aren't going to let these chimpanzees just sit out there and suffer in a sanctuary."

According to the organization In Defense of Animals, the Coulston Foundation was the only laboratory in United States history to be formally charged three times by the U.S. Department of Agriculture for violations of the federal Animal Welfare Act. The laboratory settled the first set of charges, which involved citations for deaths causes by human negligence, by paying a $40,000 fine in 1996. The other charges included numerous violations, including deficient supervision of research and inadequate veterinary care—that go to the heart of the laboratory's ability to conduct quality testing. The Coulston Foundation had also run afoul of other federal agencies.

The National Institutes of Health (NIH) had placed restrictions on the laboratory's NIH-funded testing, based largely on inadequate veterinary staffing and the death of a chimpanzee named Eason, who was involved in the testing of an artificial spinal device, resulted in yet another investigation. Eason and ten other chimpanzees were under the care of a single inexperienced veterinarian.[4] In 2002 the Coulston Foundation closed, and the Center for Captive Chimpanzee Care, founded and directed by Carole Noon, took over the facilities. The Center's purchase was made possible by an unprecedented grant of $3.7 million from the Arcus Foundation of

---

4. A chronology of events related to the continued abuse of chimpanzees at the Coulston Foundation can be found at www.vivisectioninfo.org /old/Coulston/tcfchron1.html.

Kalamazoo, Michigan, a long-time supporter of Carole's Florida sanctuary. Among the chimpanzees who were permanently retired were sixteen of the celebrated Air Force chimpanzees, who survived or who were descendants of chimpanzees used in the U.S. space program.[5] I visited the facility soon after the Center for Captive Chimpanzee Care had taken over, and I was amazed by how much Carole and her team had done. I also was appalled when I imagined how horrible the lives of the chimpanzees had been for years when they were living in filthy prison cells.

Animals and the law: Buying and selling animals as "property"

Are animals truly protected by existing laws? Many people, including legal experts, disagree on this question. The law defines animals as property, as mere resources or "things" for human use and consumption, and this means that it is extremely difficult for animals to get meaningful legal protection. Animals can almost never win when human and animal interests are pitted against each other. Just because there are laws that permit something to happen—"It's legal, so we can do it"—does not mean that no one can challenge these laws and change them as a result of open discussions. Did you know that it is possible for people to privately own great apes and that there are few regulations that these people need to comply with? This should not be possible, but loopholes in existing laws and relaxed enforcement allow it to occur. In Georgia, two severely malnourished chimpanzees were discovered in an unlit cellar living amid months of accumulated

---

5. www.primatefreedom.com/coulstongone.html.

feces. Just weeks before this terrible situation was discovered, a veterinarian had signed a permit saying that the apes' housing conditions were adequate. Fortunately, both chimpanzees have made strong recoveries since their rescue.

Here is more to think about. Animals—and not only domesticated companions—can be ordered by mail. For example, there is a publication called *The Animal Finders' Guide* from which people can order chimpanzees, monkeys, various carnivores including red foxes and wolves, bears, tigers, and camels. One needs to ask what the lives of these animals will be like in captivity in unregulated captive environments. A book called *The Animal Dealers* (Drayer 1997) exposed the horrible abuse of animals by people motivated solely by economic gain.

Changing deeply held beliefs and attitudes about animals is a very important move. Many people are working on educating the public to view animals not as property or objects, but as subjects of their own lives. The organization In Defense of Animals has a campaign called Seeds for Change devoted solely to this issue, and the lawyer and animal advocate Gary Francione has written a book titled *Animals, Property, and the Law* (1995) about the suffering of animals that results when they are treated as property.

Listening to animals and taking their points of view

How can we, as humans, begin to understand and appreciate the lives of animals who are so different from us? No animal can speak a human language sufficiently to communicate their experiences to us (although some, such as parrots and gorillas, have demonstrated the intelligent use of human language concepts). And because their bodies and senses are often quite different from ours, their experience of their reality may not be very similar to our own: for example, the noses of many animals are much more sensitive than ours, and they see and hear things at different frequencies of light and sound. Some animals fly, some swim, and others live on the edges of cliffs, in underground tunnels, or in dark caves for most of their lives. Although we can only make educated guesses about the lives of animals, if we study them carefully and try hard to understand how they live, we can make extremely good assumptions about them. Just how good our assumptions are is shown by the fact that we can predict very accurately the behavior of numerous animals as they go about their daily activities.

Let's consider my late dog buddy Jethro. Jethro had a better sense of smell than I do. The neurons in his brain are wired up differently, and the area of his brain that deals with odors is more developed than mine. Like other dogs Jethro often lifted his head to the wind to pick up odors of others who had been there, and he also spent a lot of time sniffing the ground, shrubs, and other dogs. Whereas we humans tend to rely mostly on our sight and feel that our eyes give us most of our information, for dogs it is the sense of smell that predominates, and their extremely sensitive noses mean that they experience the world very differently from the way we do. Although we would not want to put our noses into the smelly places that dogs seem to enjoy, we can appreciate that for a dog, scents evoke a rich and fascinating world.

While smell is the dominant sense for dogs, for bats it is hearing. Their ability to hear very high frequencies, or ultrasound, enables them to avoid obstacles and find prey while in flight. Humans cannot even perceive the sounds that fill the environment for bats. But we can empathize with them by understanding that they, like other animals, have their own unique perspective on life—their own way of living that is right for them.

If animals could talk

The famous philosopher Ludwig Wittgenstein once claimed, "If a lion could talk, we would not understand him." He seemed to assume that because the lion's consciousness is so different from ours, even if there were a spoken lion language, it would be too alien for us to understand. However, lions and many other animals do indeed communicate in their own ways, and if we make an effort to understand their communications, we can learn much about what they are saying. If Wittgenstein had gotten off his couch and actually watched animals, he might agree.

Just because most animals do not do things as we do does not mean that we are "better" than they are or that our perception of reality is more "true" than theirs. All living beings on earth are valuable on their own terms. Each knows and understands the world in his or her own way. It is true that we humans have unique capabilities that other animals lack. We can build cars, use computers, and fly airplanes. We can also think about abstract ideas, plan for the future, and worry about our taxes. But we cannot run as fast as cheetahs, see as well as hawks, swim like dolphins, or soar like eagles. So, rather than think that other animals are not as smart or capable as we are—that they are "less than human"—it is better to realize that being *different* is not in itself "good" or "bad." *Animals are certainly not less than human.*

Anthropomorphism: The benefits of viewing animals in human terms

In order to talk about the world of animals, we have to use whatever language we speak. So, when we want to describe what an animal may be feeling, we tend to use the same words that we would choose to describe our own human feelings or intentions. My companion dog, Jethro, might have wagged his tail and looked like he had a smile on his face, or he might have seemed to be moping around the house or run off with his tail between his legs. If you asked me how he is feeling, I might tell you he is happy or sad. Even if you had not observed Jethro directly, I am sure you would have an accurate picture of what he was doing that led me to draw conclusions about how he felt.

By saying that Jethro is happy, sad, angry, upset, or perhaps in love—that is, by using human terms to describe his emotions and thoughts—I am practicing *anthropomorphism,* the attribution of human characteristics to nonhuman animals. It is a practice that many of my colleagues object to, because they consider it unscientific. Of course, I cannot be absolutely certain that Jethro was happy, sad, angry, upset, or in love, but I have no other way to describe what he was doing and what this indicated about what he might have been feeling. In fact, I cannot really know for sure that people are feeling what *they* say they are feeling, but this would be an incredibly chaotic and disorderly world if we did not rely on at least some common sense and trust!

Anthropomorphic double-talk: Animals can be happy but not sad?

It is often assumed that anthropomorphizing causes us to draw incorrect conclusions about animals' emotions and behavior. But extensive studies by Françoise Wemelsfelder and her colleagues show that even regular folks (as opposed to trained scientists) do a consistently good job in identifying the emotions of animals with whom they interact, such as pigs

(Wemelsfelder et al. 2000). Anthropomorphism can thus be a useful tool for getting closer to and embracing the animals we study. It allows their behavior and emotions to be accessible to us. And, if we practice what I call "biocentric anthropomorphism"—that is, taking the animals' point of view by using the information that we have about the world of members of that species—we do not discount the animals' point of view.

Over the years I've noticed a curious phenomenon. If a scientist says that an animal is happy, no one questions it, but if a scientist says that an animal is unhappy, then charges of anthropomorphism are immediately raised.

A good example is the story of Ruby, a forty-three-year-old African elephant living at the Los Angeles Zoo. In fall 2004, Ruby had been shipped back to Los Angeles from the Knoxville Zoo in Tennessee because people who saw Ruby in Knoxville felt that she was lonely and sad. A videotape taken by Gretchen Wyler of the U.S. Humane Society showed Ruby standing alone and swaying. Wyler said Ruby behaved like "a desperate elephant." Sad and lonely animals often rock back and forth repeatedly. This stereotyped behavior is not normal and is characteristic of bored and distressed animals.

Wyler and others who claimed that Ruby was unhappy were accused of being anthropomorphic by people who thought that Ruby was doing just fine, both in Knoxville and again in Los Angeles. The former director of conservation and science for the Association of Zoos and Aquariums, Michael Hutchins, claimed that it's bad science to attribute human-like feelings to animals, claiming: "Animals can't talk to us so they can't tell us how they feel" (Biederman 2004). Hutchins was critical of people who claimed that Ruby wasn't doing well in captivity and was unhappy because she lived alone and had been shipped from one place to another during the past few years, forcing her to leave her friends behind.

The mayor of Los Angeles also weighed in and claimed, "She's in good spirits, and we're glad to have her back." And John Capitanio, the associate director for research at the California Primate Research Center at the University of California at Davis, made the following claim: "Do animals have emotions? Most people are willing to say they do. Do we know much more than that? Not really. . . ." Capitanio also claimed that "Animals, in some ways, are a neutral palette on which we paint our needs, feelings and view of the world." Can anyone really believe that the billions of animals who suffer at our hands are neutral palettes? If they're really unfeeling and neutral about the world, then why would researchers bother to study them in the first place? How boring that would be. And why have numerous countries banned research on sentient beings? It's precisely because animals are not neutral about how they're treated that they tell us this in myriad ways.

Hutchins went on to discount the view that Ruby was unhappy, saying: "An animal might look agitated, but it might not be. It might be playing. It might look like it's playing, but be quite aggressive." Hutchins is right that it's possible to mistakenly classify an animal's behavior, but it's wrong to imply we can never figure it out. Careful and detailed behavioral studies have shown time and again that we can indeed differentiate and understand animal behavior and how it differs in various social contexts.

Does it matter whether Ruby was happy or sad? It does. If she were shown to be unhappy, the zoo would be obligated to care for her better. Zoo officials and the L.A. mayor felt very comfortable saying she was "doing well," and Hutchins and Capitanio felt it was "good science" to rebut any claims to the contrary.

But seeing positive emotions in Ruby is as anthropomorphic as seeing negative emotions. And Hutchins and friends didn't even realize this. In fact, anthropomorphism was not really the issue; the charge was merely a smokescreen to discredit the other side. The issue was animal welfare, and the only thing to decide was, even if we can't know with absolute certainty what Ruby was thinking, whose interpretation seemed most likely, given what we know of her history and of elephant behavior?

Hutchins and Capitanio did not specifically address elephant behavior, only their ideological "foes." But those who work with elephants (mahouts) know that one ignores an elephant's "mood" at one's own peril. British philosopher Mary Midgley (1983) said it well: "Obviously the mahouts may have many beliefs about the elephants which are false because they are 'anthropomorphic'—that is, they misinterpret some outlying aspects of elephant behaviour by relying on a human pattern which is inappropriate. But if they were not doing this about the basic everyday feelings—about whether their elephant is pleased, annoyed, frightened, excited, tired, sore, suspicious or angry—they would not only be out of business, they would often simply be dead."

Inappropriate anthropomorphism is always a danger, for it is easy to get lazy and presume that the way we see and experience the world must be the only way. It is also easy to become self-serving and hope that because we want or need animals to be happy, they are. In fact, the only guard against the inappropriate use of anthropomorphism is knowledge, or the detailed study of the minds and emotions of animals.

It is essential that we try to take the animals' point of view and seek answers to the fascinating questions of how animals interact in their own worlds and why they behave the way they do. Imagine what their worlds are like to them. What it is like to be a bat, flying around, resting upside down, and having very sensitive hearing. Or what is it like to be a dog with a very sensitive nose and ears? Imagine what it is like to a free-running gazelle or deer, a wolf or coyote, living free in nature. The worlds of animals are truly awe-inspiring. We should welcome the opportunities they selflessly offer us to expand our limited human-centered perspective and learn from them.

I should stress that we need to be asking what it would be like to be a particular individual *from his or her own perspective,* not merely from our anthropocentric or human-centered view of things. Being anthropomorphic doesn't mean we ignore the animals' perspectives. Rather, using human terms to describe animal behavior allows us to understand better the behavior, thoughts, and feelings of the animals with whom we are sharing a particular experience. We can be anthropomorphic and still do rigorous science.

3

Making Decisions about Animal Use

Who Should Be Spared and Who Should Be Sacrificed?

Speciesism: Judging by group rather than individual characteristics

Speciesism, a term coined by the British psychologist Richard Ryder, reflects a prejudicial attitude, like racism or sexism, in which one judges others not on their individual characteristics but on their membership in a group—in this case, their species. People who use species membership as a basis for deciding how animals may be used by humans are called speciesists by their critics. Non-speciesists do not make that distinction—they do not use species membership to make decisions about how animals should be treated. Instead, they take into account the *individual features* of an animal.

Human superiority is often taken for granted by those who argue from a speciesist bias. They believe that humans are above and apart from all other animals—"higher" or more worthy than other animals. Many speciesists argue from a religious belief that humans are the "highest" animals because they were made in the image of God. Other speciesists hold human lives as more valuable simply because human intellectual and moral capacities are more advanced.

Many speciesists, however, place nonhuman primates such as apes on an equal footing with humans (who are also primates). These people may believe that only primates are able to experience pain. However, people taking the non-speciesist perspective realize that individuals in *many* other species experience anxiety, suffering, and pain, both physically and psychologically.

Human animals use numerous other animals in many ways, for food, research, education, entertainment, and testing cosmetics and other products. Animals such as dogs, sea lions, and dolphins have been used in warfare both to find wounded individuals and offensively to locate enemies. When humans want to expand their horizons—by building housing, shopping malls, or roads—animals are often moved out of their habitat to get them out of the way. They may even be killed: prairie dogs are routinely slaughtered to make way for human sprawl. Is it all right to move or to kill animals just so that humans can have more living space or more roads on which to drive? Many people argue that benefit to humans justifies such measures. This is speciesism in action.

There are many issues that we could raise concerning speciesism. The best way to deal with some of the most important ones is to present "thought experiments" and let you think about the questions that are raised.

Thought experiment: Humans and a dog in a lifeboat

Imagine the following situation. A small boat contains four humans and a dog. The boat is far from shore and will sink if all five individuals remain in it. One individual must be thrown overboard, even though it means certain death. You are asked to decide which individual it will be.

One easy answer—all other things being equal, which they rarely are—would be to throw the dog overboard because "he's only a dog." He will not lose as much, it is argued, because his life is not as long or full of rich experiences as those of the humans. Furthermore, the dog will not suffer as much because he will not know that he is going to be thrown over and cannot anticipate that he will drown after being in the water for a few minutes. At least that is what some people believe.

But wait—the dog will die, and this loss of life is sad and regrettable. And would not the dog's guardian also grieve and suffer the loss of her dog?

What if there were four humans—three young people and an eighty-year-old man—and a young dog who had his whole life before him? Would these facts change your mind? Would you choose to throw the old man over because he has already lived a fairly complete life and has less to lose than the younger humans and the dog?

What if the dog was your companion or one of the people was your friend?

What if there was a senile adult and a brain-damaged infant among the humans?

Would you choose to toss a murderer overboard if one were on the boat? What would it mean if all individuals have an *equal* right not to be harmed?

While this scenario is imaginary, it offers much to think about concerning how humans make decisions about human and animal lives. Indeed, one children's discussion group that I led (in Jane Goodall's Roots & Shoots) decided that no one should be thrown overboard and that there had to be a solution that would allow all the individuals to survive.

What defines a "person"?

People often use speciesist arguments to justify which animals can be used for various purposes. For example, some might say that all and only humans, regardless of individual unique characteristics, might constitute a group that is protected from harmful research. However, in 1998 the British government extended protection to all the great apes—primates belonging to the biological family *Hominidae,* which includes chimpanzees, gorillas, and orangutans as well as humans—by banning their use in medical research. This decision was speciesist, because animals of other species were excluded. It was argued that these primates deserve special treatment because of their cognitive abilities, including the capacity to be self-conscious, engage in purposeful behavior, communicate using a language, make moral judgments, and reason. Some philosophers even think that nonhuman animals who show these capacities should be called "persons."

How do speciesists draw the line between humans and other animals in determining who should be protected? They often do so on the basis of "biological closeness," or similarities to humans—similar appearance, similar behavior, or the possession of various cognitive capacities displayed by adult humans of normal intelligence. If we used these criteria, most animals would not qualify for protection. But there also are some humans who would not qualify either: for example, adults suffering from dementia and young infants do not have the necessary cognitive abilities. Would these humans then be considered "nonpersons"?

Because of individual differences within a species, a human-centered "them versus us" perspective can be difficult to apply consistently. Most of us wouldn't feel comfortable allowing

47

some animals to be considered "persons" while not allowing certain human beings to be called "persons." Instances where it is difficult to decide whether an animal is a person or whether a human is not a person are referred to as "marginal cases." Marginal cases are of great interest because there is much at stake, especially if a human being were considered to be a non-person and could then be subjected to the same experiments as nonhuman animals who also are considered to be nonpersons. For example, if being able to make plans for the future is considered a necessary condition of personhood, then humans who are incapable of making future plans would be considered nonpersons. If "personhood" is to be the determining factor in deciding which animals can be experimented on and which should be protected, then there are some very complex definitions that need to be agreed upon before legal protections can be enacted.

Evolutionary continuity

Speciesism also ignores *evolutionary continuity*, the view that evolution takes place along a continuum. Charles Darwin, the famous nineteenth-century English biologist who founded the science of evolution, stressed that in many cases, mental abilities are continuous from one animal species to the next. Darwin argued that differences in mental abilities were not differences in *kind* but differences in *degree* along a continuum. The following analogy might help show what Darwin meant: Costly Rolls-Royces and less expensive Fords are both cars. The differences between them are differences in degree—or level of luxury—and not differences in kind. By contrast, Rolls-Royces and motorcycles are different *kinds* of motor vehicles. Of course, animals are not objects, but with them we can also talk about differences in degree and differences in kind. Thus, the differences in mental abilities between wolves and chimpanzees are differences in degree rather than differences in kind. This simply means that there are many similarities in the mental abilities of wolves and chimpanzees and that chimpanzees are not 100% different from wolves. Speciesism ignores the similarities and wrongly stresses that the differences are differences in kind.

Language and tools

For many years, people decided that it was the use of language that made humans stand out from other animals. But when it was discovered that there are other animals who use language to communicate with one another, language was no longer a reliable measure of how humans are separate from other animals. Of course, animals do not speak languages like English or Spanish or Swahili, yet many use their own complex languages consisting of vocalizations or movements to tell their kin what food is available, where they are traveling, how they are feeling, or what they need.

There was also a time when it was thought that only humans made and used tools, so this ability was used to separate humans from other animals. But when Jane Goodall, studying chimpanzees at the Gombe Stream in Tanzania in October of 1960, observed David Graybeard (and later other chimpanzees) making blades of grass into tools for extracting termites from a mound in order to eat them, she revealed that tool use is not unique to humans. Now it is known that many animals, including birds, use tools.

Many researchers continue to insist that we humans are separate from other animals. They point to activities that only humans engage in and then use these activities to claim that humans are not only smarter than other animals but also unique. However, animals are unique too; they can do many things that we cannot do. Is a dog who can pick up the scent of another dog from a great distance, or a bat who can find prey by using high-pitched sounds, so special that its life is more valuable than that of humans who cannot perform these behaviors?

The main point is that all animals have to adapt to being who they are and where and how they live. Each may have special skills that others lack, but none is "better." There are no nonhuman animals who can program computers or practice law. But there are no humans who can fly like birds, swim like fish, run as fast as cheetahs, or carry as much weight (relative to their own body weight) as ants.

So, are humans unique? Yes, but so are all other animals. The important point that needs much discussion focuses on the question "What differences make a difference?" Are there any differences between individuals that make it all right to use or exploit one animal rather than another? If we respect all life forms, then it will be hard for us to draw the line between those individuals whom we are allowed to use, harm, or kill, and those whom we may not. But, from the practical point of view, especially if you agree that *sometimes* it is all right to use animals, at times you must make a decision that implicitly values the life of one individual animal over another. This applies to you, the reader, and to researchers and policymakers.

Animal intelligence

Since humans have more advanced intelligence than other animals, people often argue that this makes it all right to use and to exploit animals with lower intelligence. However, recent research on animal intelligence has revealed some eye-opening surprises in this regard. Frequently, differences in *degree* are found where differences in *kind* were expected before the research was conducted.

Researchers who study animal intelligence and animal thinking are called *cognitive ethologists*. They ask various questions about the ways in which animals show that they are smart: Do animals think or plan for the future? Do they try to deceive one another? Do they display signs of culture, such as making and using tools?

What are some specific behavior patterns that indicate that an individual is smart? Being "smart" means showing flexible behavior in new and unpredictable situations, as well as anticipating the future and making plans. When an environment changes and animals need to adjust and fine-tune their behavior to new situations, or when a novel solution is needed, then activities suggestive of problem solving and planning are seen in several different species.

Animals are said to be smart if they perform such tasks as:

- counting objects
- forming concepts in which differences or similarities are recognized
- being able to elude clever predators
- locating hidden food
- making and using tools
- deceiving others
- using complex forms of communication

Quite a few species of animals display these and other skills. For example, let's look at a few varieties of animal communication.

Studying the ways animals communicate is a useful way to learn about the workings of their active minds. Prairie dogs and vervet monkeys use different alarm calls to warn one another about the approach of different predators. While animals such as birds will utter a single or fairly stereotyped warning cry if a predator is approaching, only certain animals make *different* warning sounds to indicate what *kind* of predator is present. Dr. Con Slobodchikoff, a biologist at Northern Arizona University, found that Gunnison's prairie dogs have different alarm calls for hawks, coyotes, domestic dogs, and humans. Likewise, Robert Seyfath and Dorothy Cheney at the University of Pennsylvania discovered that vervet monkeys have different calls for snakes (pythons) who hunt on the ground, carnivorous mammals such as leopards, and martial eagles hunting on the wing. They found that vervet monkeys use different warning calls to alert other group members to the specific type of immediate danger. Other group members respond to these calls appropriately (even when predators are unseen): they flee into trees and climb out onto small branches when they hear a leopard alarm call, move into thick vegetation when they hear an eagle alarm call, and stand on their hind legs and look around when they hear a snake call.

Alex, an African grey parrot studied by Irene Pepperberg, understands the concepts of "same" and "different" and can answer questions about the number, color, shape, and composition of objects presented to him. For example, Alex is presented with plastic objects—three yellow, one purple, and one red—and one piece of green wood, and then he is asked, "What material green, Alex?" he answers, "Wood." And when asked, "How many yellow?" Alex says, "Three." Certainly, research on Alex proves that calling someone a "bird brain" is not necessarily an insult. Before Pepperberg's groundbreaking research, it was thought that parrots only mimicked human speech and had little or no understanding of what they were uttering or of concepts such as "same" and "different." Now we know that

African greys have remarkable cognitive abilities and can connect many human words with their meanings. There is also a lot of exciting research done on great apes' capacity for language. Roger and Debbi Fouts, at Central Washington University, have studied a chimpanzee named Washoe and many other chimpanzees for the past four decades. Washoe was the first animal to regularly use a human language—American Sign Language (ASL, the primary sign language of the U.S. deaf community)—and other chimpanzees later succeeded at it as well. These chimpanzees can communicate this way not only with people but with one another, and they will even sign to one another during play when humans are not around. Chimpanzees' vocal organs are physically unable to produce words, but Kanzi, a male bonobo (pygmy chimpanzee), learned to communicate by pointing to a keyboard on which there are numerous symbols called lexigrams. When he is asked a question, he answers by pointing to a symbol. Kanzi can understand sentences spoken to him by his mentor, Sue Savage-Rumbaugh, even ones that are illogical, like "Put the ball in the microwave."

Are such examples of parrot and ape intelligence only seen in pampered captive animals who live with humans? Not at all. Groups of Kanzi's relatives, wild bonobos living in dense forests, have been observed by researchers who did not interact with them in experiments in which there was as close contact as there was with Savage-Rumbaugh. After splitting up into small groups during the day, these bonobos could track and locate one another by using signs that symbolize where they are heading. When trails cross, the leaders stamp down vegetation or place large leaves on the ground pointing in the direction of travel. Trail notes are left only where trails split or cross, where there could be some confusion about direction, and not at arbitrary points. When all members travel together, trail markings are not used.

By following the trail signs that bonobos had left, Savage-Rumbaugh was able to find her way to the group at the end of the day. Clearly, bonobos are communicating with one another using trail symbols. They seem to anticipate what other bonobos will do after seeing and processing the information contained in the symbolic trail markers.

The ability to deliberately deceive others is another sign of animal intelligence. Many examples of this occur in relation to food. An animal might hide food when other animals are around, distract their attention by looking away from the food, or lead them away from the food. When rhesus monkeys find food, they will often withhold this information and not call others to the area, something that they will do when there isn't any food around. A wolf will often cache (conceal remains of a kill by burying it for later retrieval) when no other members of the pack are watching: Why share if you do not have to?

Who is smarter?

We have seen that different species display different kinds of behavior, and such differences are the rule rather than the exception. But behavioral variations in and of themselves are of little use as a basis for deciding which animals should be protected or how animals should be protected. That is, these variations should not be viewed as being "good" or "bad" or as proving that animals are "higher" or "lower" on a scale of life.

Now, how does speciesism come into play when we examine animal intelligence? Are chimpanzees "smarter" than mice or dogs, for example? If we believe that this is so, then we need to be very clear about why. We need to be clear about what we mean when we claim that the social lives of chimpanzees are more complex than those of mice or dogs, or that chimpanzees are able to solve more complex or difficult problems, or that chimpanzees show more flexible patterns of behavior in response to environmental changes—that they can change their behavior in order to survive in changing conditions. It is also important to remember that mice and chimpanzees each do well in their own worlds, and neither would do well in the others' habitat. Many people, if they *had* to make a choice between harming a mouse and harming a chimpanzee, would probably not have much trouble deciding to spare the chimpanzee. Nonetheless, their decision should not be made conveniently along species lines, merely by arguing that the chimpanzees are "higher" than mice. Individual characteristics need to be taken into account. For example, while it would still be a difficult decision, one might choose to do invasive research on a chimpanzee who is in a terminal coma rather than on a live, sentient mouse.

"Smart" and "intelligent" are words that are often wrongly used to compare animals of different species. Dogs do what they need to do to be dogs—they are dog-smart in their own ways. And monkeys do what they need to do to be monkeys—they are monkey-smart in their own ways. Neither is necessarily smarter than the other. The misunderstanding and misapplication of the notions of smartness and intelligence can have significant and serious consequences for animals, especially if they are thought to be dull and insensitive to pain and suffering.

Thought experiment: A healthy mouse or a sick chimpanzee?

To try to make moral decisions by drawing boundaries at the species level—judging by the behavior patterns typical of a species rather than evaluating the individual animal—leads to many difficulties. Suppose, for example, you had to decide which was more ethical: experimenting on a healthy mouse or on a severely mentally impaired chimpanzee in a persistent vegetative state. Or suppose there were an experiment where you had to restrain the physical movements of an animal. Which animal would you subject to this treatment if you had to choose between a healthy, active mouse and a severely physically disabled chimpanzee, one that could not move about much anyway? In decisions such as these, it is not entirely reasonable to compare a *normal* mouse to an *abnormal* chimpanzee. For example, if some procedure could be carried out harmlessly on a chimpanzee but would require harming a mouse, then the mouse should be spared. Thinking through imaginary examples such as these can help people to come to terms with the difficult issues at hand on a case-by-case basis. In other words, we have to consider the specific situations of individual animals and not merely say that chimpanzees should *always* be spared in preference over mice.

Too often, the use of animals in science is determined on the basis of their similarity to or difference from human beings. In other words, if a species is very different from us, such as a frog, we think it is more acceptable to experiment on it and even kill the individuals involved, rather than use a species belonging to the great apes, who are much more like us. Why do some people feel comfortable subjecting animals to experimental research that will harm or kill them, but refuse to use humans for this type of research? If the animals are vastly different from us, then the results of the experiment may not reliably apply to humans. However, humans are more similar to humans than they are to any other animals, and it truly is a compromise to use other animals rather than humans for research intended solely to benefit people.

Why do people disagree about these questions? This is very difficult to explain, but there are a few reasons that are usually given. First, some people believe that humans are special animals who are superior to all other animals because only humans have been created in the image of God and only humans are rational beings—that is, they can reason. Although it is correct to say that humans are unique, it is also correct to say that every individual animal is in some ways unique, and that is true even of identical twins.

Other people simply feel that animals are here for humans to dominate and to control because, they believe, we are more advanced evolutionarily, smarter and more conscious, and we therefore suffer more than other animals. Yet others believe that humans are permitted to use animals for whatever they want as long as there are human benefits. For these people, the ends (human benefits) justify the means and the costs (the use and abuse of animals).

A belief that runs throughout all of these views is that humans are "higher" or "better" than other animals. Although there are numerous differences between humans and other animals, it is clear that in many important ways, humans and animals are united in a single web of life: "we" are one of "them," and "they" are one of "us."

The Great Ape Project: Granting legal rights to apes

An important movement known as the Great Ape Project (GAP) was launched in 1993 (see Cavalieri & Singer 1993). As a contributor to Cavalieri and Singer's book on the project and as a participant in meetings in which the GAP was promoted, I strongly supported its goal of admitting great apes to the "Community of Equals," in which the following basic moral rights, enforceable by law, are granted:

1. the right to life,
2. the protection of individual liberty, and
3. the prohibition of torture.

In the GAP, the notion of "equality" does not refer to any specific actual likeness between humans and apes, but means equal moral consideration.

Some people do not think that the Great Ape Project goes far enough, because of its speciesist concentration on great apes to the exclusion of other animals. I agree. But the Great Ape Project had to start somewhere, and beginning with animals who would generate the least resistance was probably the correct place to begin: most people are sympathetic to the idea of granting legal protection to these animals with whom we feel a natural kinship. While many people might be willing to enact legislation in favor of the great apes, many would not want to grant rights to dogs, cats, birds, mice or other rodents typically used in research, fish, crocodiles, lobsters, or ants.

Going beyond apes: The Great Ape/Animal Project

When I first contributed to the GAP, I wanted to include other animals in this project and to rename it the Great Ape/Animal Project (GA/AP), and to expand membership in the Community of Equals. In the GA/AP it is assumed that all individual animals have the right to be included in the Community of Equals. *All life is valuable and all life is to be revered.*

Clearly, I believe we must include more species in discussions of animal protection and animal rights. As we learn and understand more about the animals with whom we share this planet, we will gain greater appreciation and respect for all life than we have at present. The study of animal behavior helps us to learn about how animals experience their own worlds and about their capacities for experiencing a broad range of emotions ranging from joy and pleasure to pain and suffering. And, as I've mentioned before, there are always surprises in science—for example, discovering that mice behave with empathy for other mice and that whales possess spindle cells in their brains, which are important for processing emotions. Keeping our minds and hearts open to the cognitive and emotional capacities of other animals is the best way to move into the future as we ponder how we interact with the individuals with whom we share our planet.

4

Animal Sentience

Do Animals Experience Pain, Anxiety, and Suffering?

Are animals conscious?

Many people want to know whether animals are conscious. Are they truly aware of their surroundings? Are they perceptually conscious? If being "conscious" means only perceiving the things around them with their senses, then animals are obviously conscious at least on a perceptual level. Of course, numerous animals, including humans, act like robots—mechanically, by instinct or programmed habit—in many situations, so it would be wrong to think that humans *always* act with a "higher" awareness.

There are different degrees of consciousness. In addition to perceptual consciousness, there is also what some call a higher degree of consciousness, namely self-consciousness, an awareness of who you are in the world. For example, as long as my brain works normally, I know that I am Marc Bekoff, and I can be fairly sure that there are no other Marc Bekoffs who are exactly like me, with the same set of past experiences. If something happens to me that I like or dislike, I know it is happening to *me* and not to you.

It is also possible that I may not know *who* I am, but I may be fully aware of something happening to my body. If I received a blow to my head and sustained a brain injury, I might not know my name, or who I am, but I would be able to feel the pain that was caused by my injury, and it would be wrong to make me suffer just because I do not know my name. There is little doubt that many other animals know when something painful happens to their body. Even if they do not know their name, they are able to experience that "something bad is happening to this body."

It is obvious that self-awareness has evolved in our close kin such as chimpanzees and in familiar animals such as dogs and cats. Indeed, experimental research has shown that a few species besides humans can recognize themselves in mirrors, which reveals some degree of self-awareness. For example, chimpanzees and various monkeys have been shown to use their mirror image to groom parts of their bodies (such as their teeth and their backs) that they cannot see without the mirror. Some also look into a mirror and touch a spot that was placed on their foreheads while they were sedated and unaware that the mark was placed there. This self-directed behavior suggests that the great apes and certain monkeys might have a sense of their own bodies, that this is "me." Bottlenose dolphins have also demonstrated self-recognition in a reflective surface. Most recently, in 2006, researchers at the Bronx Zoo discovered that elephants display this awareness as well. An Asian elephant named Happy repeatedly touched her trunk to a white X marked on her forehead, which she could only see by looking in the mirror. While these animals use visual cues, it is known that dogs and mice, for example, use odor to differentiate self from others. It is important to remember that animals use different senses than we do and that visual cues are not the only ones used in self-awareness.

If we pay attention to some basic and well-accepted biological ideas, it is impossible to justify the belief that we are the only species on this planet in which individuals are self-aware. Although we are very different from other animals, it is unlikely that we are the only species that is self-aware and able to think, feel pain, experience anxiety, and suffer. As we observed earlier, Darwin showed that there are many connections among different animals, that there is *continuity* in evolution. Even if we are very different from dogs or cats, there is no reason to think that dogs, cats, and many other animals are not conscious and self-aware in their own species-typical ways.

Sentience: Consciously feeling pleasure and pain

Animals who are conscious and aware of pleasure and pain are said to be *sentient*. Put another way, *sentience* means being responsive to sense impressions. And a sentient animal is one for whom "feelings matter," as my colleague John Webster, a veterinarian in Bristol, England, puts it. As I have emphasized before, in order to learn about animals, we must try to understand their own worlds—what it is like to be a gorilla, a dog, a bat, a robin, or an ant. Even though their own perceptual experience and the way they sense the world around them are usually very different from ours, they can still be conscious in their own ways and also experience pain and suffering in their own ways. *Their own pain and suffering are no less important than our pain and suffering.* Sentience is very important to consider when we make decisions about how to use animals because sentient animals experience pain, and just like us, they do not like it.

Animal emotions

Many animals experience fear, joy, happiness, humor, shame, embarrassment, resentment, jealousy, rage, anger, love, pleasure, compassion, respect, sadness, despair, and grief. Human observers have identified elephant joy and sadness, chimpanzee and goose grief, and happiness and love in dogs. Joyce Poole, who has studied wild elephants for more than two decades, comments: "It is hard to watch elephants' remarkable behavior during a family or bond group greeting ceremony, the birth of a new family member, a playful interaction, the mating of a relative, the rescue of a family member, or the arrival of a musth male [a male ready to mate], and not imagine that they feel very strong emotions which could be best described by words such as joy, happiness, love, feelings of friendship, exuberance, amusement, pleasure, compassion, relief, and respect" (Poole 1998).

Animals' emotional states are easily recognizable. Just look at their faces, their eyes, and the way they carry themselves. Even people with little or no training in observing animals tend to agree about what an animal, especially a mammal, may be feeling. And their intuitions are borne out, because they can rather accurately predict an animal's future behavior based on their interpretation of its emotional state.

The expression of various moods in animals raises many challenging questions about their emotional lives. As examples, I will consider grief and joy.

Many animals display profound grief at the loss or absence of a close friend or loved one. Konrad Lorenz writes: "A greylag goose that has lost its partner shows all the symptoms that [developmental psychologist] John Bowlby has described in young human children in his famous book *Infant Grief*... the eyes sink deep into their sockets, and the individual has an overall drooping experience, literally letting the head hang..." (Lorenz 1992).

Jane Goodall observed Flint, a young chimpanzee, withdraw from his group, stop eating, and die of a broken heart after the death of his mother, Flo. Here is Goodall's description:

> Never shall I forget watching as, three days after Flo's death, Flint climbed slowly into a tall tree near the stream. He walked along one of the branches, then stopped and stood motionless, staring down at an empty nest. After about two minutes he turned away and, with the movements of an old man, climbed down, walked a few steps, then lay, wide eyes staring ahead. The nest was one which he and Flo had shared a short while before Flo died. . . . in the presence of his big brother [Figan], [Flint] had seemed to shake off a little of his depression. But then he suddenly left the group and raced back to the place where Flo had died and there sank into ever deeper depression. . . . Flint became increasingly lethargic, refused food and, with his immune system thus weakened, fell sick. The last time I saw him alive, he was hollow-eyed, gaunt and utterly depressed, huddled in the vegetation close to where Flo had died. . . . the last short journey he made, pausing to rest every few feet, was to the very place where Flo's body had lain. There he stayed for several hours, sometimes staring and staring into the water. He struggled on a little further, then curled up—and never moved again. (Goodall 1990)

Sea lion mothers, watching their babies being eaten by killer whales, wail pitifully, anguishing their loss. Dolphins have been seen struggling to save a dead infant and mourn afterward. And elephants have been observed standing guard quietly over a still-born baby for days, their heads and ears hanging down, moving slowly. Joyce Poole has witnessed the undeniably real phenomena of grief and depression in orphaned elephants. Young elephants who saw their mothers being killed often wake up screaming. Animals also experience immense joy when they play, greet friends, groom one another, and are freed from confinement. They even seem to enjoy just watching others having fun. Joy is contagious.

Animals tell us they are happy by their behavior—they are relaxed, walk loosely as if their arms and legs are attached to their bodies by rubber bands, smile, and go with the flow. They also speak in their own tongues—purring, barking, or squealing in contentment. Dolphins chuckle when they are happy. African wild dogs greet one another with squealing, propeller-like tail wagging, and bounding gaits. When coyotes or wolves reunite, they gallop toward one another whining and smiling, their tails wagging wildly. They are jubilant upon meeting, licking one another's muzzles, rolling over, and flailing their legs. When elephants come together after being apart, there is a raucous celebration as they flap their ears, spin about, and emit a "greeting rumble." They are so happy to see one another.

Joy abounds in play. Animals become deeply immersed in the activity and show their delight by their acrobatic movements, gleeful vocalizations, and smiles. There's a feeling of incredible freedom in the flow of play. Violet-green swallows soar, chase one another, and wrestle in grass. I once saw a young elk in Rocky Mountain National Park run across a snowfield, jump in the air and twist his body while in flight, stop, catch his breath, and do it again and again. Buffaloes have been seen playfully running onto and sliding across ice, excitedly bellowing *gwaaa!* as they do so.

As I point out in my book *The Emotional Lives of Animals* (2007), numerous studies demonstrate that there are neurochemical bases for why play is enjoyable, and that the same chemical changes occur in both animals and humans during play. A boy and his dog wrestling in the yard are not only both playing—they both are getting the same pleasurable feelings from doing so. Neurotransmitters such as dopamine and perhaps serotonin and norepinephrine are important in the regulation of play, and large regions of the brain are active during play. Rats show an increase in dopamine activity simply anticipating the opportunity to play. Opioids are also linked to play. These neurochemicals are related to feeling relaxed or "socially comfortable," a condition important for facilitating play.

The more we study animal emotions and the more open we are to their existence, the more we learn about their fascinating emotional lives. Surely, it would be narrow-minded to think that humans are the only animals who have evolved and experience deep emotional feelings.

Do animals suffer?

One of the most basic questions people are concerned about is whether animals suffer and feel pain. To experience pain, an individual must have at least a simple nervous system, such as that of a worm. Pain includes a range of unpleasant sensations that serve to protect animals from physical damage or threats of injury. For example, when animals are bitten hard, they move away from the animal biting them. Although the animal can't tell us in words what is happening, we conclude from this behavior that the animal is seeking to avoid a painful sensation.

There is no doubt that many animals experience pain. Veterinarians have developed a pain patch for dogs coming out of surgery, because they are convinced that dogs feel pain and suffer from medical procedures. Indeed, we have all heard dogs yelp when they step on a nail, catch their tail in a door, or are bitten too hard. As a significant step in the right direction, in 1998 the University of Tennessee College of Veterinary Medicine established the first Center for the Management of Animal Pain to improve methods of preventing and treating pain in animals.

While there are obvious differences in the behavior of individuals belonging to different species, there are also differences in the behavior of individual members of the same species: some may be more sensitive to pain and discomfort than others. However, in and of themselves, behavioral patterns may mean little for arguments about animal protection. Many animals experience pain, anxiety, and suffering, physically and psychologically, when they are held in captivity or subjected to starvation, social isolation, physical restraint, or painful situations from which they cannot escape. Even if it is not the same experience of pain, anxiety, or suffering undergone by humans— or even other animals, including members of the same species— an individual's pain, suffering, and anxiety matter.

In everyday life, the experience of pain is unavoidable. Pain serves many useful functions and contributes to survival. Humans and animals lacking pain systems by accident of birth or disease tend to have shorter lives.

Which animals feel pain?

While researchers cannot say for sure which species feel pain, there is much evidence that animals who many people thought could not feel pain, such as fish, do know the experience of hurting.

Fish have nerves similar to those that are associated with the perception of pain in other animals. Fish show responses to painful stimuli that resemble those of other animals, including humans.[1] Even some invertebrates—animals without backbones such as insects—seem to experience pain and also possess nerve cells that are associated with the feeling of pain in vertebrates—animals with backbones such as humans and other mammals. Whether some insects actually feel pain is not known, but because they might, some people believe that they should be given the benefit of the doubt. Humans should assume that animals can experience pain and treat them accordingly. The octopus, an invertebrate with a large central nervous system and complex behavior, has been given the benefit of the doubt in Great Britain. In 1993 it was added to the Animals (Scientific Procedures) Act of 1986 that regulates the use of animals in scientific research. Octopuses are now protected along with mammals, birds, reptiles, amphibians, and fish.

The emotional experience of pain is something of which every individual is aware. While we all try to avoid painful situations, some pain may be unavoidable or even beneficial for an individual, such as the pain experienced from receiving an injection that helps to cure a disease or prevent rabies.

René Descartes, the influential sixteenth-century French philosopher and scientist, believed that animals were like robots, simply programmed to react out of instinct but not able to think or feel pain. Today we no longer believe that animals are mechanical "things." Yet some people still think that animals other than humans, even our close relatives such as gorillas and chimpanzees, do not experience pain. When scientists do admit that other animals feel pain, it is usually only those animals who look like us or behave like us who are most likely to be granted the

---

1. See www.newscientist.com/article.ns?id=dn3673.

capacity to feel pain. People might also accept that familiar companion animals, including canaries, parakeets, dogs, and cats, and perhaps urban wildlife such as deer and raccoons, can feel pain. But when it comes to animals they dislike, such as cockroaches or snakes, or ones they want to kill for sport or food, like fish or chickens, they are not willing to concede that these creatures suffer too. Once again, speciesism is at work.

Is animal pain different from human pain?

When a lobster, an invertebrate with a much simpler nervous system than ours, is casually dropped alive into a pot of boiling water, how can we tell whether it feels terrible pain the way a person would under similar circumstances? A major problem in this debate over which animals truly feel pain is that many animals may not experience pain exactly the way we do. Different animals might have more tolerance for some situations and less for others. Because an animal like a lobster is not like us, some people think lobsters do not feel pain, because their pain is not like our pain. However, there are differences between species, and it is wrong to assume that dogs, cats, birds, fish, ants, and lobsters will behave just as humans do in painful situations. Remember, we do not do many things in the ways that other animals do, and there is no reason to think that we will all feel pain or respond to it in the same way. Different species differ in many ways, including how they perceive and feel pain and how they react to it. The lobster cannot scream and pull itself out of the boiling water, but that doesn't mean it isn't being tortured. Let's be open to a variety of findings and not make speciesist assumptions.

5

Animal Rights and Animal Welfare

What implications follow from the conclusion that animals can indeed feel pain and experience deep emotions? If animals are able to suffer, then we must be careful not to cause them intentional and unnecessary pain and suffering, because it is morally wrong to do so. Of course, giving my dog Jethro a painful injection to cure his lung infection or to reduce the pain he occasionally felt from his badly arthritic leg would be permissible. The major point is that our starting must be that it is wrong to cause intentional and unnecessary pain unless there are compelling reasons to override this principle that are for the benefit for the individual animal.

The difference between animal rights and animal welfare

While some people believe that it is acceptable to cause animals pain if the research will help humans, there are others who argue that this should not be done even if humans might benefit from the research. If we want to use animals for testing or research, but this use would cause them pain, then we must look for other research methods that do not cause suffering to living beings. People who believe that we are allowed to cause animals pain are not necessarily completely indifferent to animals' suffering. They may insist that we should not to cause them *excessive* or *unnecessary* pain, and argue that if we consider *animal welfare* or well-being, then that is all we need to do. These people are called *welfarists*. Animal welfare is different from *animal rights*. The *rightists* believe that it is wrong to cause animals any pain and suffering, and that animals should not be eaten, held captive in zoos, subjected to painful experiments, or used in most or any research. They believe that animals have certain moral and legal rights that include the right not to be harmed.

According to Gary Francione, a lawyer and animal rights advocate, if we agree that an animal has a "right" to have its interest protected, then the animal has a claim, or entitlement, to have that interest protected *even if it would benefit us to do otherwise*. Humans would then have an obligation to honor that claim for other voiceless animals just as they do for young children and the mentally disabled. For example, if dogs have a right to be fed, you have an obligation to make sure that any dog under your care is fed. If a dog has a right to be fed, then you are obligated not to do anything to interfere with feeding her. Of course, you might prevent her from feeding on garbage or something that might harm her, but this isn't what I'm referring to.

Professor Tom Regan, a professor of philosophy at North Carolina State University, is often considered the originator of the modern animal rights movement. His book *The Case for Animal Rights* (1983) attracted much attention to this area. Advocates who believe that animals have rights stress that animals' lives are valuable in and of themselves, not valuable just because of what they can do for humans or because they look or behave like us. Animals are not property or "things," but rather living organisms, subjects of a life, who are worthy of our compassion, respect, friendship, and support. Rightists expand the borders of species to whom we grant certain rights. Thus, animals are not "lesser" or "less valuable" than humans. They are not property that may be abused or dominated at will. Any amount of animal pain and death is unnecessary and unacceptable.

By contrast, people who support animal welfare do not think that animals have rights (Francione 1996). They believe that while humans should not abuse or exploit animals, as long as we make the animals' lives physically and psychologically comfortable, then we are adequately taking care of them and respecting their welfare. Welfarists are concerned with the quality of animals' lives. But welfarists do not believe that animals' lives are valuable in and of themselves, or that it is just because animals are alive that their lives have worth.

Welfarists believe that if animals experience comfort, appear happy, experience some of life's pleasures, and are free from prolonged or intense pain, fear, hunger, and other unpleasant states, then they are doing fine and we are fulfilling our obligations to them. If individuals show normal growth and reproduction, and are free from disease, injury, malnutrition, and other types of suffering, they are doing well.

This welfarist position also assumes that it is all right to use animals to meet human ends as long as certain safeguards are used. They believe that the use of animals in experiments and the slaughtering of animals as food for humans are all right as long as these activities are conducted in a humane way. Welfarists do not want animals to suffer from any unnecessary pain, but they sometimes disagree among themselves about what pain is "necessary" and what humane care really amounts to. But welfarists agree that the pain and death animals suffer is sometimes justified because of the benefits that humans derive. For them, the ends justify the means—the use of animals even if they suffer because the use is considered to be necessary for human benefits.

Nonetheless, animal welfare groups, such as the Humane Society of the United States, have contributed important efforts to successful campaigns to protect animals. A recent victory occurred in May 2007, when President George W. Bush approved new legislation requiring stronger punishments for those who promote or encourage the brutal practice of blood sports such as dog fighting and cockfighting.

Although there are significant points of difference between rightists and welfarists, it's important to acknowledge that both agree that in reasoning about moral choices, we must avoid the bias of speciesism. If we are to succeed in making life better for animals, we humans must find ways of harmoniously resolving our philosophical differences about how best to accomplish the goal.

Do domesticated animals deserve less than their wild relatives?

One position that many scientists take in deciding which animals may be used in research favors domesticated animals, such as companion dogs and cats, rather than wild animals. Their reasoning is that humans owe less to these animals. I believe that treating domestic animals less respectfully than their wild counterparts is unjustified. J. Baird Callicott (1980), a philosopher who has written extensively about animal and environmental ethics, once claimed: "Domestic animals are creations of man. They are living artifacts." He also wrote, "They have been bred to docility, tractability, stupidity, and dependency. It is literally meaningless to suggest that they be liberated." Callicott believes that domestic animals have been bred to be stupid, but gives no indication of what measures he uses. He does not realize that simply because animals do things in ways that may seem "stupid" by human standards, this is no reason to demean the manner in which they adapt to their own worlds. I would argue that there are no stupid animals—only narrow-minded humans who do not take the time to learn more about the animals they call stupid.

Because some people believe that domestic animals are creations of humans and therefore less deserving of our compassion and respect than their wild relatives, they argue that wild animals should be assigned higher moral status than domestic animals. People who think that domestic animals have a lesser moral status than their wild relatives usually present a more permissive standard of human conduct toward domesticated animals. Is this fair to domesticated animals whom we have created and many of whom have developed a deep trust in us? Domestic animals certainly can and do experience pain and suffer, and there is no evidence that their pain and suffering are very different from, or less than, those of closely related wild relatives.

Far from having no moral obligation to protect domesticated animals, perhaps humans actually have special obligations to do so. Domesticated animals may suffer more psychologically than their wild counterparts when their expectations are not met in their interactions with humans. The philosopher L. E. Johnson (1991) summed it up nicely when he wrote: "Certainly it seems like a dirty double-cross to enter into a relationship of trust and affection with any creature that can enter into such a relationship, and then to be a party to its premeditated and premature destruction." Some field-workers indeed believe that the animals they study come to trust them.

Researchers observe the animals and do not otherwise interfere in their lives. For example, Jane Goodall believes that her relationships with the chimpanzees she intensively studied can best be described as one of "mutual trust." Trust and expectations of certain types of behavior on the part of animals are brought forth by the ways in which humans have interacted with them in the past, and not, of course, by a signed formal contract.

6

Utilitarianism

Trying to Balance the Costs and Benefits of Using Animals

Weighing costs and benefits

In the real world, many people practice welfarism. They think of animals with respect to how they may serve the needs of humans: how they may be used in research, for food, or for amusement or entertainment. Because this view of animals is so prevalent, it is worth looking closely at how welfarism works.

People who consider animals' usefulness to humans are called *utilitarians* and they practice *utilitarianism*. The modern-day champion of utilitarianism as it relates to animals is Peter Singer, an Australian philosopher who teaches at Princeton University and is the author of the book *Animal Liberation*.

Utilitarians typically believe that neither animals nor humans have rights. The only criterion by which they decide whether an action is right or wrong is the principle of utility, or use-value. Will the action produce the greatest utility, defined as the maximum benefit, advantage, or happiness to human beings? Utilitarians believe that a dog, cat, or any other animal may be used by humans as long as the *costs* to the animal—the pain and suffering that the animal experiences—are less than the *benefits* to humans that are gained by using the animal.

Singer has written that the best course of action is the one that has the best consequences, on balance, for the interests of all those who are affected by a particular decision to do something or not to do something. It is important to note that the interests of animals must be given equal consideration with those of humans, and that animals and humans have an interest in avoiding suffering.

When utilitarianism is applied to animals, it is very similar to welfarism. The only rule, and it is not a moral rule, is that it is all right to use animals if the relationship between the costs to the animals and the benefits to the humans is such that the costs are less than the benefits. Utilitarians may argue that it is all right to use one million mice in cancer research to save only a single human life, because the costs to the mice (being made ill and losing their lives) are less than the benefits to the humans who might benefit from a treatment that was developed using the mice. Or they may believe that it is all right to keep gorillas or other animals in cages in zoos, because the costs to the animals are less than the educational benefits to the humans who are thus enabled to learn about the gorillas' lives.

A major problem with utilitarianism is how to calculate costs and benefits. How do we decide that the pain, suffering, and lives of one million mice cost less to the mice than the benefits that are gained by one or more humans? Why not balance one million mice with one hundred humans, or one million mice with one hundred thousand humans? Because it is humans who are making the decisions about costs and benefits, there is always the chance that there will be some bias in favor of humans. That risk is exactly why many people are not satisfied with utilitarianism: because it is humans who make the decisions, it is pretty easy to make the equation always come out in favor of the humans. An animal's interest can be ignored if it benefits us to do so.

According to the standard version of utilitarianism, first offered by the English philosopher Jeremy Bentham (1748–1832), what really matters is pleasure or pain. Bentham was very interested in animals and wanted them to be considered in moral decisions made by humans. Because of his concern for animals, he wrote that the question is not "Can they *reason*?" nor "Can they *talk*?" but "Can they *suffer*?" It did not really matter to him if animals could think or if they were smart; rather he was concerned with whether or not they could suffer. It is the costs associated with suffering that need to be considered when deciding how costs and benefits are balanced. Utilitarians who follow Bentham's ideas judge an action as right if it leads to greater pleasure than pain. In other words, people should aim to maximize pleasure (the benefit) and minimize pain (the cost).

Utilitarianism has a lot of appeal because it is very flexible. But the flexibility of utilitarianism may also mean that the utilitarian does things that are at odds with accepted morality. One way in which people argue against utilitarianism is to show that it can lead to conclusions such as that it is all right to harm animals, break promises, tell lies, and even kill a human so that you can give her home to some worthy cause—if the costs are less than the benefits, or if the consequences for all involved have a positive effect that is greater than the negative effect.

Many utilitarians believe that the pain and suffering of most animals could never equal the benefits that humans gain from animal use. Therefore, animals start out with a disadvantage, and usually remain behind humans when costs and benefits are decided. Some people think that the life of a chimpanzee is more valuable than the life of a mouse or a shrimp, so they may argue that fewer chimpanzees should be used than mice, for example, in biomedical research. But trying to assign an exact value to the life of an animal is very difficult, and in the end, most people make decisions as if human life is always more important than animal life.

Thought experiment: Utilitarianism at work

Let us try an exercise similar to the "Humans and a Dog in a Lifeboat" thought experiment that we considered in our discussion of speciesism in chapter 3. Imagine that you need to decide whether it is all right to use mice or chimpanzees in a research project on lung cancer, the results of which *might* save human lives. I say "might" because using animal models in studies of human disease does not always work to produce solutions to a problem (I will discuss this later). However, the results of the research could turn out to help numerous humans. Or, perhaps the results might help mice and chimpanzees but not humans; or it might produce information that is beneficial to chimpanzees and humans but not to mice.

You need to decide if it is all right to use one thousand mice or one thousand chimpanzees in the project. There is no guarantee that any humans, mice, or chimpanzees will benefit, but you do know that the mice and chimpanzees will experience pain and might even die from the disease, or have to be killed in order to analyze their organs and cells. What would you decide? Here are some options, and I will let you formulate others.

You might simply decide that it really does not matter how many mice or chimpanzees are used, even if the results turn out to have no benefits for humans. Or you might decide that even if there are no human benefits, it is all right to use a thousand mice but only one hundred chimpanzees, because chimpanzees are smarter than mice, because chimpanzees will suffer more than mice, or because chimpanzees are smarter and will suffer more than mice. Of course, at some time you will have to defend why you chose the numbers one thousand and one hundred.

But there are other possibilities. Perhaps your best friend would decide that we need more information about whether there is any chance that the research will benefit humans and until we know this, we should not use *any* mice or chimpanzees. Or perhaps she will decide that only mice but not chimpanzees can be used.

Still, there are other options. Would it make a difference to you if your mother, father, sister, or brother might benefit from the research? Perhaps it would, and then you might decide that researchers may use any number of mice or chimpanzees—or any other animal—if there is *any* chance that your family member would benefit. Perhaps if your best friend were suffering from this disease you would make the same decision.

As I said previously, because there are so many factors that enter into figuring out how costs and benefits are determined, and because there are no strict rules that can be used to make decisions about costs and benefits, it is the flexibility of utilitarianism that makes it so hard to apply.

Who benefits?

Let us list some of the variables that play a role in using utilitarianism:

1. Who is the person who makes the decision?
2. Who are the people who might benefit?

3. Which animal species are to be used?
4. How are the animals to be used?

One question that needs to be added to this list (but often is not) concerns possible *benefits to the individual animals* who are used, or benefits to other members of the same or other species. Will any animals benefit from the use? Perhaps the individual mice or chimpanzees who are used will benefit from the research if they survive the procedures and do not suffer pain and injuries from which they cannot recover. Perhaps other mice and other chimpanzees will benefit from the pains, suffering, and death of other mice and chimpanzees. So, it is for the good of the species that some individuals suffer or are killed. Some people believe that it is permissible to trade off the life of an individual for the good of their species, and that sort of reasoning is considered in deciding costs and benefits.

This discussion brings us to our next topic. Should we be concerned about animals as *individuals* or only as groups, especially *species*? To discuss this question, I will briefly consider a topic that is receiving much attention nowadays: the reintroduction of animals, such as wolves, into areas where they lived in the past but were exterminated because of human persecution. Reintroduction is an important topic because it raises many questions concerning the interests and rights of individuals versus species, and what, if anything, we owe to endangered species. It also raises the issue of global biodiversity: Should humans strive to maintain biodiversity, the great variety of species on the planet? Or should we allow events (such as extinction) to take their course with as little human interference as possible?

7

Species, Individuals, and the Reintroduction of Wolves

Who Counts?

Reintroducing animals into their wild habitats

Let us now look briefly at the topic of *reintroduction* of animal species into areas where they used to live. This discussion will be useful in tying together the topics we have already considered: speciesism, animal rights, animal welfare, and utilitarianism. In particular, we will ask whether reintroduction programs can balance the interests of a particular *species* against the needs and well-being of the *individual* animals that are placed in a wild habitat.

Humans are constantly making choices about how to use other animals, and some of these are extremely difficult decisions. The animals themselves have no say in these decisions. They depend on our goodwill and mercy.

Many people believe that it is individual animals who are important in our moral decisions about how they can be used. These people would say that the species to which an individual belongs is not important. Remember that people who support animal rights believe that each and every life is important and valuable. Therefore, *we must make all our moral decisions based on an individual's own characteristics and not on the species to which it belongs.* Recall also that speciesists—those who use species membership to make decisions about how animals should be used by humans—lump individuals into a group; as a result, the unique interests or needs of the individual animal fail to be addressed, and as such they lose their identity.

A question of great interest that also generates a lot of controversy concerns whether or not animals should be reintroduced into areas where they have lived in the past. Reintroduction programs usually involve animals who are endangered or have become extinct in the wild. By reintroducing them to their habitats, biologists hope to develop sustainable populations that will thrive in the future. In the United States, one of the most ambitious reintroduction programs involves grey wolves who used to live in many areas, including Yellowstone National Park (portions of which are located in Wyoming, Montana, and Idaho). Wolves in Yellowstone and other areas were hunted and killed by humans in the past. As a species, wolves were almost exterminated in the lower forty-eight states of United States, and they were officially listed as "endangered" by the U.S. government. However, as of the writing of this book, there is a move to delist wolves (that is, take them off the endangered list) in the Rocky Mountain and Great Lakes regions of the United States.[1]

Many people, including conservation biologists, politicians, and even some ranchers, think that we should correct the actions of humans in the past and reintroduce wolves to areas where they once lived. Others disagree, either because they are concerned that wolves will kill livestock and other animals, or because they feel that nature should take its course and that

---

1. www.jacksonholenews.com/article.php?art_id=1386.

what humans do is part of the natural process. Of course, if wolves have been exterminated and then reintroduced, reintroduction too must be considered part of the natural process. One can't have it both ways.

Should individuals suffer for the good of their species?

What are some of the events surrounding reintroduction? Frequently, wolves who are to be reintroduced into an area are taken from another region where they live and moved to the new area. In a sense, they are kidnapped from where they and their ancestors have lived. Sometimes individuals suffer or die when they are trapped, during transport, or when they are held in cages before being released into the new area. *Is it fair to use these individuals—who may suffer or die—for the good of their species?* Is it fair to move individual wolves from areas where they and other wolves have thrived and place them in areas where they might not have the same quality of life, just because we believe that the move will benefit the wolves as a species in the future? Some people say that since the animals will die eventually anyway, it is all right to move them. Of course, just because an animal, nonhuman or human, may eventually die in one way does not justify killing them sooner in another way.[2]

There are other questions that need to be considered. Individual wolves are sometimes kept in captivity for purposes of breeding, in order to help expand the wolf population and ensure that litters survive. They live in cages and never get to

2. I have discussed many of these issues in an essay titled "Jinxed Lynx" that I wrote concerning the reintroduction of Canadian lynx back into Colorado. See www.umich.edu/~esupdate/library/99.3-4/bekoff.html.

roam freely like other free-ranging wolves. Is it all right to deprive these individuals of their freedom and natural way of life in order to benefit the species?

These are very difficult questions. Humans are trying to make decisions for animals who have absolutely no say in their future. We are their surrogate decision makers, imposing *our* values on *their* lives. *Should these individuals suffer and perhaps die for the good of their species?* While most humans can make decisions about whether to use their own lives for the good of our species, other animals cannot. Many of these decisions are made because it is humans who want wolves to roam once again in areas such as Yellowstone. Because of the human desire to see wolves or know that the species is thriving, individuals are sacrificed for the good of their species.

The story does not end here. What about other predators in the habitat where the wolves are being reintroduced? Animals who usually kill the same animals for food that wolves do might now experience increased competition for food. They may also face more direct threats from the wolves. For example, wolves are killing coyotes very frequently in Yellowstone now that wolves have been put back there. Coyote packs are disappearing from areas where they have lived for decades, either because coyotes are being killed or they are being forced to move by the presence of wolves. Robert Crabtree and Jennifer Sheldon, who have conducted long-term research on coyotes in the Lamar Valley in Yellowstone, report that wolf-killed coyotes during the winters of 1997 and 1998 resulted in a 50% reduction in coyote numbers. Coyote pack size also decreased from an average of six coyotes to four. Allowing wolves to kill coyotes suggests that wolves are more valuable. Do you agree that this is so? Why or why not?

It also is important to consider large species such as elk, who, in the absence of wolves, were very rarely killed by predators.

Now they will become "wolf food." Is it all right to impose new pain and suffering on them while trying to improve the lot of the wolves?

Redecorating nature: Whose interests are more important, ours or the animals'?

Clearly, there are many difficult questions that need to be considered. As we have seen, one of the major questions is: *when is it all right to override an individual's life for the good of its species?* It is likely that we will face this and other questions in the future, as conservation agencies along with local people attempt to re-create animal communities in areas where they once lived. We must be very careful when we attempt to "redecorate nature."

I raise these questions *not* because I am against reintroduction programs. Indeed, the Yellowstone project appears to be successful in that wolves are breeding and the population is growing. Rather, I ask them because the repercussions are often more complex than people realize, so that we need to look very closely at the issues. When trying to restore ecosystems, we should be concerned with the animals who are involved, not only with our own human-centered goals. Individual animals should not suffer and die unnecessarily because of what we want. We must also take into account the fact that ecosystems continue to develop in the absence of predators, and reintroduced animals will therefore be entering a changed habitat. It may turn out in some cases that it would be unwise to try to regain what was lost, as further problems would arise. Furthermore, it might be impossible to re-create what once existed simply because times and conditions change, and one can never reproduce what once was.

The costs of trying to re-create ecosystems by reintroducing animals might be too great for the animals involved, because of how they have to be treated—trapped, marked with tags so that individuals can be identified, and moved from one place to another. During the relocation process, families and friendships may be broken up as well. Moreover, it is unlikely that the programs will be successful, because the animals, especially those reared in captivity, are not prepared for life in the wild because they haven't had to take care of themselves or gather food on their own. There might not be enough suitable habitat in which they can thrive. Humans living in the area might not accept reintroduced animals such as wolves or other predators because they are afraid they might attack people or livestock.

Such problems certainly have plagued wolf reintroduction programs. Indeed, the Yellowstone program is in jeopardy because people get upset when wolves behave as the natural predators they are. Wolves do kill livestock and do roam from the locations where they are released. If the animals are going to pay with their lives for living their evolved lifestyle, then reintroduction programs cannot be easily justified.

Thought experiment: The last wolf on earth

Reintroduction programs raise questions concerning how we make decisions to use animals belonging to different species. Here is a challenging scenario for you to consider, substituting an animal who is personally meaningful to you. A friend of mine, the philosopher Ned Hettinger of Clemson University, during numerous discussions about animal rights, environmental ethics, and biodiversity, often asked me to imagine the following hypothetical question.

Suppose I am driving down the road and I am fated to hit and instantaneously kill an animal that suddenly dashes under the wheels. Now imagine further that I actually have a choice: the animal I will hit with my car can either be *the last wolf on earth or my companion dog Jethro.* What a terrible dilemma! Which one would I choose?

My answer always is that I would choose to kill the last wolf.

However, I often wonder whether I am wrong to make this choice. Am I too self-centered? What about the fact that if Jethro dies, there will still be many other dogs, but if I kill the last wolf on earth, then a beautiful species will be extinct? Do I owe something special to the wolves? Yet, there also will never be another Jethro; he is a special friend who is near and dear to me, and he means more to me than any other animal, even the last wolf—who, if not pregnant, will never produce more wolves anyway. My friendship with Jethro makes it impossible for me to be impartial. Friendship and trust are important values that cannot be left out of this discussion.

There are many very difficult questions that require further discussion: What if the last wolf was indeed pregnant? What if there was a group of wolves, or what if the choice involved another domestic dog whom I did not know personally? My answer remains that I would still choose to save Jethro's life. While I am really not sure what I would do if the dog involved was not Jethro, I might very well spare the dog if she were one whom I knew, and if I also knew that she had a caring human companion who would grieve her loss.

So, would you allow a dog—even your dog—to be killed to save wild animals? Do we owe our domesticated companions less than we owe wild animals? Would your answer be different if it were not your own companion animal or if the wild animals were rare and endangered? If you would sacrifice your dog for the sake of saving wild animals, perhaps animals who are endangered, can you explain why maintaining biodiversity is so important as to justify that decision?

I will return to some other questions about reintroduction programs in the next chapter. It is important to stress that reintroduction programs are not bad ideas and are not always ill-fated. Rather, there are numerous questions that need to be given serious thought, and our thinking about them often gets distorted by the emotional appeal of reintroducing beautiful animals back into areas where they once lived and the feelings that are evoked in us by seeing wolves and other wonderful animals in the wild. It's true that it feels great simply to know that they are out there. But at what cost?

8

Zoos, Wildlife Theme Parks, and Aquariums

Should Humans Hold Animals Captive?

What are zoos good for? Most people think that they promote education about wildlife. But is there any evidence that this is so? Would it surprise you to learn that the Association of Zoos and Aquariums (AZA) admits: "Little to no systematic research has been conducted on the impact of visits to zoos and aquariums on visitor conservation knowledge, awareness, affect, or behavior"?[1]

Zoos have existed for a very long time. Although the modern type of zoo is only a few hundred years old, even in ancient Egypt, wealthy people are known to have kept collections of wild and exotic animals. The first zoos in Europe opened in the late 1700s. In the United States, the first European-style zoo opened in 1874 in Philadelphia, modeled after the London Zoo. The first public aquarium in the United States was opened even earlier, in 1856, by P. T. Barnum, the famous circus owner. Early zoos were primarily for the amusement of humans and

---

1. AZA, Executive summary: Visitor learning in zoos and aquariums, www.aza.org/ConEd/MIRP/Documents/VisitorLearningExecutive Summary.pdf.

not for the benefit of the imprisoned animals. They were essentially living museums.

In the United States, the Association of Zoos and Aquariums (AZA), founded in 1924, is responsible for inspecting zoos, "wildlife" theme parks, and aquariums (collectively referred to as zoos). (I put the word *wildlife* in quotation marks because I question whether animals in cages are truly wild in the same way as their relatives who live free in nature.) If these institutions meet AZA standards, they are approved and accredited by the AZA. There are only 216 accredited zoos, theme parks, and aquariums in the United States and more than 2,000 licensed zoos that are not accredited by the AZA,[2] but it is difficult to estimate their numbers accurately. These unaccredited zoos, theme parks, and aquariums are legal, and the AZA has no say in how they operate and the way they treat animals.

It is important to stress that zoos vary greatly in quality. Some experts feel that many zoo exhibits are antiquated because the cages do not provide animals much enrichment or the floors are hard concrete rather than grassy; only about one-third could generously be called "enriched" or "naturalistic." A former zoo director once confided to me that he would like to improve 95% of the exhibits he has visited in American zoos. While there are some zoos that are exerting every effort to make the lives of animal residents the best they can be, there are numerous zoos that are of very poor quality. If we are to consider whether or not it is ethically desirable for zoos to exist, we must take into account the fact not only that *all* captive animals have compromised lives and are being kept without their permission, but also that there are some zoos where the animals simply are treated horribly. To give just one example, an elephant named

---

2. www.aza.org/Accreditation/AccreditList.

Maggie has languished for years in the Alaska Zoo, being forced to live alone and having to endure snow and cold during Alaska winters. However, on the positive side, the Bronx Zoo and zoos in Detroit, Chicago, San Francisco, and Philadelphia will be phasing out their elephant exhibits because they have come to realize that they cannot meet the social and physical needs of these magnificent mammoths.

The problem of "surplus" animals

In addition to the fact that captive animals lead unnatural lives that often are tragically impoverished,[3] some zoos sell, trade, donate, or loan unwanted or "surplus" animals to animal dealers, auctions, hunting ranches, unidentified individuals, unaccredited zoos, and game farms whose owners actively deal in the animal marketplace. The fact is that most zoo animals are like museum specimens and will never be freed from captivity. The animals are treated as mere property, their fate dependent on their dollar value. From 1992 to the middle of 1998, about one thousand exotic animals were sold as live merchandise. Alan Green (1999) has reported on the vast underground trafficking in rare and endangered species in the United States. Other animals are also sold or traded regularly. There are about 250 tigers in AZA-approved zoos but about six or seven *thousand* "pet" tigers confined in horrible conditions. Bears who have been assigned to petting zoos often find themselves shipped off to market as food after they are no longer useful. Green's stories and pictures will bring you to tears, and we should be grateful for his bringing these issues to the forefront for public scrutiny.

---

3. An excellent four-part series on zoos appeared in the *San Jose* (California) *Mercury News,* February 7–10, 1999.

Naturalistic exhibits and environmental enrichment: Trying to make captive lives better

Nowadays, many zoos have what they call naturalistic exhibits, and wildlife parks provide animals with areas in which to roam that simulate their natural habitats. There is an attempt to meet the physical and behavioral needs of the caged animals by providing them with an environment that as closely as possible resembles their natural environment, from which they may have been taken or in which their wild relatives still live. Despite these efforts, animals confined to such exhibits do not lead natural lives. For example, while American brown bears in captivity spend about the same percentage of time being active as wild bears, most of this time is spent pacing, not engaging in a natural activity such as foraging.

There is a movement to have animals live in naturalistic groups. Wolves often are kept in groups that resemble wild packs, and animals who are more solitary are allowed to live alone and have places into which to escape or hide if they want to get away from other animals or from human spectators.

Some zoos attempt to provide captive animals with enriched environments that stimulate and challenge them and reduce boredom from being in the same place with little to do day in and day out. Enrichment programs give animals control over their environment and often provide them with choices of different activities in which to engage. Nonetheless, all individuals in zoos have their freedom of movement constrained, and even in the best of enriched environments, there are limits on the behavioral choices that can be made. Much enrichment is really designed for the human visitors' enjoyment, since enriched environments typically do not resemble the natural environment of the caged animals.

Many different types of enrichment have been used. Different species have different needs, and there are individual differences within species (for example, age and gender may influence what works). The main goal of enrichment programs is to give animals more control of their lives and have them "work" to occupy their time. Enriching animals' lives can be accomplished in numerous ways, including providing safe and secure places for resting, sleeping, and escaping from unwanted intrusions by cage mates and humans, allowing individuals of social species to live in pairs or larger groups that resemble natural groups, making them work for meals by providing frozen food or by scattering or hiding it, providing natural flooring or terrain rather than hard concrete, spraying various odors in cages, making it possible or easy to exercise, providing larger cages (although this is not always enriching), and increasing the complexity or diversity of their social and/or physical environments. Moderate levels of stress that tax the animals might be beneficial, especially for individuals who are to be reintroduced to the wild. For example, it might be helpful to make individuals work hard for food if food is going to be difficult to obtain in the wild.

While enrichment programs do not directly address the question of whether or not humans should hold other animals captive, the very few captive individuals who have the opportunity to experience enriched environments do seem to be more content or happier than those who do not. Compared with discontented individuals, those animals who are in a good psychological health—happy and content—do not engage as much in behaviors such as stereotyped pacing, in which an individual repeats the same pattern of movement over and over again (for example, a bear paces back and forth and, when she switches direction, sways her head in precisely the same pattern), "cage rage" and self-mutilation, rocking back and forth, and unusually high levels of fear and aggression. Instead, they engage in various types of play, have good appetites, and do not suffer from the abnormally high levels of stress, anxiety, or disease as their less fortunate kin.

Nonetheless, captive animals whose lives are enriched, just like animals in smaller cages, have their freedom of movement restricted, and their lifestyles are very limited. Individuals simply do not have the opportunity to live like their wild relatives, roaming freely and pursuing the lives that nature intended them to live. Their range of choices is very limited and they have no control over their own destinies.

Public opinion about zoos

There is much disagreement about whether zoos should or should not exist. A 1995 Roper poll showed that almost 70% of Americans are concerned about the well-being of animals in zoos. It's unlikely that existing zoos will close in the immediate future, and the live animal specimens who are kept in cages are not going to be killed (to put them out of their misery) or released into the wild. This simply is not possible, and it would be unethical to kill the animals or to release animals who might not know how to live outside of captivity without human assistance. As mentioned earlier, unwanted and "surplus" animals also need to be dealt with. Often they are housed in cages away from the main exhibits or are sold or traded.

The results of a study conducted in the late 1990s are interesting to consider when discussing people's reactions to visiting zoos. It was discovered that children notice similarities between humans and animals, whereas adults see differences. Children feel a kinship with many animals. The study also suggested that what children get from going to zoos is less about

the animals than about their own relationships with their ac-
companying adults. Furthermore, children frequently see how
horrible zoos are and often express it later in life, although not
at the time of the visit. As adults they express sorrow for the
confined animals and see them as bored creatures.

A recent study by Raymond Ings, Natalie Warren, and
Robert Young of 200 visitors to the Edinburgh Zoo in Scotland showed all visitors said it was all right to feed live insects
to lizards if it was done off-exhibit and 96% said it was all right
if on-exhibit; 72% of the people agreed with live fish being fed
to penguins on-exhibit and 84.5% if done off-exhibit. Only
32% agreed to a live rabbit being fed to a cheetah on-exhibit,
whereas 62.5% agreed to this done off-exhibit. In general,
females were more likely to object to the feeding of live ver-
tebrate prey. Clearly, behind some of this thinking was the
speciesist assumption (conscious or not) that there is a hierarchy of species, some being "higher" and others "lower." Many
people thought it was fine to feed live prey because it was "natural." If they disagreed with feeding live prey, it was because it
would upset them or their children. Ethical issues did not seem
to count for much at all.

Education, conservation, biodiversity, and endangered species

Two common reasons given to justify the existence of zoos include *education* and *conservation*. Some people believe that
zoos are good because they educate people about animals in
general and also about animal species that they would otherwise never get to see. However, Michael Kreger, at the Animal
Welfare Information Center, found that the average visitor
spends only from about thirty seconds to two minutes at a

typical exhibit and only reads some of the informational signs about the animals. A number of surveys have shown that the predominant reason people go to the zoo is to be entertained. In one study at Edinburgh Zoo in Scotland, only 4% of zoo visitors went there to be educated, and no one specifically stated they went to support conservation. There is very little evidence that much educational information is learned and retained that will help the animals in the future.[4]

Some people defend the existence of zoos because they might serve to keep individual animals of rare, threatened, or endangered species alive when the habitat of these individuals has been destroyed. However, it has been estimated that about 50%–70% of orphaned gorilla infants who are taken into captivity will not survive. The figures are similar for orphaned gorilla infants and juveniles who are released from captivity back into the wild. Living in captivity does not prepare individuals for the conditions they will face when they are on their own in the wild.

Sometimes zoos are defended as a place to care for individual animals with the intention that they (or perhaps their offspring) will be released into the wild sometime in the future. The purpose here is to help preserve or increase populations of species that are endangered in the wild. Thus, some people believe that zoos are valuable because they will help maintain biodiversity, by preventing some species from going extinct. They argue that without zoos, biodiversity will decrease as species die out. Thus—according to this argument—zoos potentially can be important in conservation efforts by keeping animals in safe places and then releasing them into the wild.

The problem with this idea arises when the animals' habitat is not preserved for them: if people use the land for human

---

4. See Animalearn Fact Files, Animals in Entertainment, #11.

purposes while the animals are held in captivity, there will be no suitable place for them to be released into. This happens quite often. Indeed, most conservation biologists agree that *habitat loss* is the major cause for losses of biodiversity. There are too many people and too little land for animals to thrive and survive. The situation is not getting better. Remember that in Kenya it is estimated that wild lands are disappearing at a rate of 2% a year. Jane Goodall has repeatedly told audiences around the world that more habitat is needed in order to protect the endangered great apes. The same can be said for a number of other species, including wolves. The main reason why there is so little suitable habitat is because there are too many people.

Zoos actually do little to increase biodiversity. While some zoos make serious efforts in the conservation arena, few zoos actually have conservation programs, and in those that do, only a small percentage of the budget is spent on them. In a period of ten years, the San Diego Zoo reported that it spent $55 million on public relations but only $17.6 million on wildlife conservation studies.

There is little evidence of success for release/reintroduction programs involving animals who have been former residents of zoos or their offspring. Although successful reintroductions have been performed for Arabian oryx (an antelope species) and perhaps golden lion tamarins (a New World monkey in Brazil), not many other programs seem to have made any difference. Since 1900, of about 145 reintroductions involving a total of 126 species and approximately 13 million individuals born in captivity, only 11% (16 programs) have succeeded in that the animals who have been reintroduced reproduce and produce viable offspring who then go on to reproduce on their own. In 1995, Benjamin Beck, then Chair of the American Zoo and Aquarium Association's Reintroduction Advisory Group, lamented that "we must acknowledge frankly at this point that there is not overwhelming evidence that reintroduction is successful." Beck also noted in 1996 that we just do not know enough to have successful rehabilitation and release programs of apes in captivity. And Terry Maple, director of Zoo Atlanta, has stated: "Any zoo that sits around and tells you that the strength of zoos is the SSP [Species Survival Plan] is blowing smoke" (quoted in Croke 1997). Thus, zoo's ability to save species is not a present-day reality.

As the environmental philosopher Dale Jamieson observes in his essay "Against Zoos" (1985), zoos basically are places where people can go to see animals, a place to go on a weekend outing for entertainment. They can eat popcorn while they watch the animals, and some may even torment animals by banging on their cages and making noises that scare them. There is really no evidence that people learn very much about animals that they remember after they leave the zoo, and there is no support for the claim that people donate much money or time to help animals after they have seen them in zoos, wildlife parks, or aquariums. Watching wildlife videos in the comfort of home would be more effective for learning about animals and for making people more sensitive to the plight of captive animals.

Jamieson also argues that if zoos truly wanted to use some animals for release or reintroduction, they would limit the animals' contact with people, would provide them with large ranging grounds that resemble natural habitats, and might have to prepare the animals to kill food in ways that viewers would find shocking. The primate specialist Roger Fouts (1997) believes that if zoos and wildlife theme parks truly cared about animals, they would make the well-being of animals a higher priority than public viewing. Of course, this would most likely mean that money would stop flowing in and zoos would face financial problems. Nonetheless, Fouts has an important point: if people who run zoos say that the animals come first, then they should put their words into action on the animals' behalf.

Zoos as businesses: The dollar speaks

The existence of zoos and wildlife theme parks raises numerous important and difficult questions. Many ethical concerns arise because zoos are businesses whose bottom line centers on money. It costs an enormous amount of money to bring animals into captivity and to keep them there. It has been suggested that the money used to capture, transport, and keep animals in cages would be better used to do research to learn more about their lives in the wild and to conserve their habitat.

How animals are kept in zoos and what people get to see in zoos is influenced by the available money. Large sums are spent on public relations and not on the animals. Susan Davis (1997), in a well-researched book on the theme parks of Sea World, points out that Sea World's version of nature—the images of nature that are represented to the public—is a manufactured, corporate point of view. As a profit-making entertainment, she says, Sea World is designed not only to amuse consumers but also to communicate a carefully planned message to silence our concerns about the environment: "Sea World isn't so much a substitute for nature as an opinion of it, an attempt to convince a broad public that nature is going to be all right." Davis also concluded that "Sea World is a machine that profits by selling people's dreams back to them—dreams of a happy family, congenial public places free of fear, a peaceful community. . . ." But most of the theme park's customers really do not believe it, except for a short-lived moment. Sea World personnel also manipulate what "news" the public is exposed to. Announcements of new animals and new animal exhibits are much more likely to draw media attention than are animal rights demonstrations or the deaths of animals.

Vicki Croke notes: "The zoo is not a window on nature but rather a prism that bends the light according to the culture it is set in." Both the design of zoo exhibits and the ways in which zoos use their money reveal much about our culture's view of animals—what we value them for and whether we regard them as objects to be used by us or as living beings who are valuable in their own right.

Animals get the blues in zoos

Zoos, wildlife parks, and aquariums, even the best of them, are mostly examples of human exploitation and domination of animals, just as are circuses, rodeos, and most recreational hunting and fishing. If the gates of zoos were left open, there would be no animals in them after a very short while.

It is indisputable that many individual animals really do get the blues in zoos. They get bored, pace about, often engage in self-destructive behavior (such as biting themselves and pulling out their fur), and frequently become unhappy and depressed. They get cage rage. As Vicki Croke concluded: "While the zoo can be an intriguing place to visit, it can be an awfully boring place to live."

Thought experiment: Questions about animal captivity

After reading this brief background, what do you think about zoos and wildlife parks? Are there any benefits to the animals that justify humans keeping them in cages or in tanks of water where their freedom is compromised? Make a list of what you think are the good aspects and the bad aspects, and think about how you would make zoos better for the animals who are there.

- Do you think zoos should continue to exist, or should they be phased out? Why or why not?
- If you believe zoos should exist, do think they should only be for animals who were born in captivity? Or is it all right to capture animals in the wild for the purpose of exhibiting them in zoos?
- From what you have read or seen, do you think there is any evidence that wild animals in captivity miss the life they used to have?
- Do you think it is all right to keep an animal in captivity even if there is very little chance it will ever be released back into the wild? Or is it only all right to keep an animal captive if it *definitely* will be rehabilitated and released back into its habitat?
- Some meat-eating animals in captivity need to be fed live animals in order to survive. This raises an ethical issue, since the zookeepers then have to either kill animals for food or allow them to be killed by their predators. Do you think it is all right to kill individual animals, or allow them to be killed, in order to feed the exhibited zoo animals? Does the *species* of the animal to be killed affect your answer to this question? Would you allow, for example, the killing of invertebrates such as insects but not the killing of mammals? Why or why not?

Someday the zoo as we now know it will disappear or be replaced by a more enlightened facility for taking care of animals who need our help. But as long as zoos do exist, it is essential that we try as hard as we can to make them the best that they can be and to make the lives of all captive animals as rich and complete as possible. If humans must play the role of guardians and protectors of animals, then we owe them unconditional compassion, support, and respect.

9

Should Humans Interfere in the Lives of Animals?

A broad range of questions must be tackled whenever we, as a society, critically examine the ways in which we interfere in the lives of animals. This interference takes many forms, ranging from using animals for our own needs or removing them from situations that we deem threatening to our interests, to trying to help them and protect them from harmful influences.

Is the wild really the best place for animals to live? Or is it a dangerous place where they may suffer from diseases, injuries, starvation, and attacks by predators? Should we as human beings intervene and protect them from "nature's cruelty"? Do we have a moral *obligation* to do so? Or does our interference only make things worse? Is it better for them to live freely and as nature intended, even if it means some hardships for both individuals and species? What about the problems that animals encounter as a result of human actions? Is it our responsibility to do something to make up for the pain that we have inflicted on animals? For answers to these and related questions, we look not only to science but also to the field of moral philosophy, the study of ethics.

Moral responsibility

Moral philosophy distinguishes between *moral agents* and *moral patients*. Moral agents are defined as those individuals who are capable of actions that they know are "right" or "wrong." Moral agents are responsible for their actions and have certain obligations to treat others in certain ways. Most adult humans are moral agents. Corporations and nations may also be considered entities who have the responsibility of a moral agent. But other individuals—including infants, the legally insane, people in a coma, or those mentally incompetent adults with severe disabilities such as retardation or dementia—cannot be held responsible for their "right" or "wrong" behavior. These people are not moral agents, but moral patients. For example, a baby cannot understand that it is wrong to take or destroy someone else's property. Similarly, a patient with Alzheimer's disease is not morally responsible if he hits someone in a moment of confusion or agitation.

Where do animals fit in? Can an animal be a moral agent? Most people realize that animals do not know "right" from "wrong" or "good" from "bad." When animals do something that humans would call "nice"—for example, caring for baby animals or interfering in a fight on behalf of a friend—we cannot say that they *know* they are being nice. When they do something that we would call "bad"—for example, wolves killing a farmer's cow—it is not accurate to say that they are doing something "wrong," because they are unaware of the moral value of their behavior. For these reasons, philosophers refer to animals as moral patients, not moral agents.

The case of a rare white Bengal tiger who killed a zookeeper at the Miami Zoo is an example of some of these issues concerning species differences in knowing right from wrong. Often in such cases, where a human being is killed, the animal is put to death by the authorities. In this case, it was decided that the tiger would not be destroyed, because "the tiger was just being a tiger."[1] Those who made this decision recognized that he was not responsible for his actions, because he did not know right from wrong. Recall from chapter 7 that after wolves were reintroduced to Yellowstone Park, people often wanted to *kill* them for "being a wolf" because they preyed on livestock.

Over the past few years, animals who attack people are not put to death if it's clear that they are not to blame for the assault. This also has been true for the rare occasions on which an elephant harms or kills a person who is responsible for its well-being. Cases are usually evaluated individually because each presents a unique set of circumstances. Thus, when a zookeeper was killed at the Denver Zoo by a jaguar in early 2007, zoo officials said they had no choice but to kill the jaguar because it was the only way to get him off the keeper. What is important, though, is that case-by-case evaluations do not always result in the animals being killed.

If animals become widely recognized as moral patients, this will have important implications. As human moral agents, we have responsibilities and obligations toward moral patients. In the imaginary case of the baby who destroyed someone's property, responsible adults are obliged to make sure that the baby is not punished for this innocent act. Similarly, if a dog walks in to a pet shop and steals some treats, there is no reason to punish her, for she is not a moral agent.

If we agree that animals have rights, then as moral patients they have the right to receive certain kinds of treatment from us, including not punishing them for actions for which they are not responsible and providing them with medical care when

---

1. *Rocky Mountain News,* June 7, 1994, p. 3A.

they need it. This is why, whenever humans interfere in the lives of wild animals, it is important to determine whether these intrusions can be justified. Are they fair? Are they the right thing to do?

Why do we interfere in wild animals' lives?

There are many reasons that people give for intruding into the lives of wild animals. Some of these reasons reflect deep concern about helping wild animals, while others are superficial and self-serving. As an example of the latter, a director of a Colorado aquarium attempted to justify keeping fish in tanks by claiming: "Fish have a very small world.... You can think of it as they are getting three square meals a day and free health insurance." As I have mentioned, there is much research showing that fish feel pain and suffer, so we cannot assume that confining fish in a tank is pleasurable for them. Also, the claim that the world of fish is very small reflects a human-centered view of other animals' worlds. The worlds of many animals are very large, diverse, and complex; we may even say that for *every* animal, its own world is big and important to itself. Individual humans' worlds are fairly small and narrow compared to those of many other animals.

So, for whose benefit will this facility provide? Certainly not the animals'. Thanks, but fish do not need more tanks. Furthermore, if fish have such small worlds and uninteresting lives, why should anyone pay to go see them? With friends like this in the zoo business, animals do not need enemies. Francis Crick, the English scientist who won the 1962 Nobel Prize for his work on the structure of DNA, believes that "it is senti-mental to idealize animals" and believes that life in captivity is better—longer and less brutal—for many animals than life in the wild. My reply is that to say we are doing animals a favor by keeping them in cages or tanks is narrow-minded *anthropocentric*—human-centered—speciesism. If captivity is so wonderful and if confined animals are so lucky as to get free meals, health insurance, and protection from nature's perils, why not incarcerate people? See how many people would volunteer. This line of reasoning can easily lead to the conclusion that if people truly want to be humane, we should place all animals in captivity or slaughter all wildlife humanely before they succumb to one of nature's horrible deaths.

Those people who argue that the wild is not the ideal state for an animal because animals suffer from diseases, injuries, starvation, predation, and intrusion by humans in the wild, feel that what humans provide for captive animals is better than what nature provides. But this view leans far to the side of human-centered control and management. Animals evolved in nature, and we should respect this fact. Yes, life can be tough out there, but it is all too easy to claim that because life is tough "out there," we are really doing animals a favor by keeping them "in here" and trying to enrich their impoverished lives.

Let's remember that animals did not evolve in cages, and animals in cages do not get to roam free or make choices about how to live, or face the trials and tribulations of being wild. Wild animals do experience pain and suffering, and their lives are not as glamorous as you might think from watching a nature special on TV. Nonetheless, they are free and are able to live the life of a free individual.

Is a wolf in a cage still a wolf?

Because of the many restrictions on the lives of captive animals, people who are against keeping animals in captivity believe, for example, that a wolf in a cage is not truly a wolf. Of course, the animal is still a wolf, but it does not have the freedom to live the life of a wild wolf. What you basically see in a cage is a caged wolf. That individual does not have the opportunity to live in a natural social group of family and friends, bond with youngsters, hunt, starve, suffer from disease, or possibly be killed by a human. But that is what it is all about to be a wild wolf. That is how they (and other animals) got to where they are now. Their behavior evolved in the wild.

It's true that wild animals may be confronted with situations that bring them pain and suffering such as disease, predation, and aggression. But except in unusual circumstances, I do not think that wild animals should be interfered with. Supposedly there is a joke going around the zoo world that animal rightists would shut down the wild if they witnessed the savagery out there (Croke 1997). I doubt this is true. Most people I know who support the rights position certainly wish that wild animals did not suffer from nature's perils, but they would not support programs that take animals out of the wild and put them into captivity to protect them from nature's ways.

The philosopher Paul Taylor has written much about this topic and developed what he calls the "rule of noninterference" (Taylor 1986). According to this rule, humans have a duty "to let wild creatures live out their lives in freedom" because intrusions into "the domain of the natural world . . . terminates an organism's existence as a wild creature." While it may seem that a wolf in captivity is better off than a wolf in the wild who is starving because of natural cycles of prey or because she is a subordinate member of her pack, once even a starving wolf is brought into captivity she remains a wolf only because of her species membership. She is no longer a wolf in the sense of a wild being who lives the life of a typical member of her species.

We also may bring more pain and suffering to individuals' lives than they would endure in the wild by taking them into captivity, although there may be different types of pain and suffering in each location. For example, with rare exceptions, the life of a tiger is not improved by putting him in a zoo. Although his food will be provided for him, hunting has played a large role in the evolution of tigers and is essential to a tiger's way of life. In the zoo, he is thus deprived of one of the most meaningful activities of his existence. His movement will also be severely restricted, and for animals who typically roam in search of food and shelter, captivity produces an impoverished existence. Furthermore, it is not at all clear that captive animals live longer than their wild counterparts or that they are healthier. While captive and wild apes typically show considerable similarities in weight, there seems to be a greater risk for captive males to suffer from obesity compared with wild relatives. This may be due to stress, inactivity, or boredom.

James Kirkwood (1992), a British zoologist, presents thoughtful views on the well-being of wild animals and considers such questions as whether we should intervene on behalf of free-living wild animals, and if so, to what extent and how it should be done. While Kirkwood recognizes that there are many different views on these important matters, he claims: "Most would probably agree that when wild animals are harmed by man's very recent (in evolutionary terms) changes to the environment (such as oil spills, power lines, roads, and environmental contamination) there is a reasonable case, on welfare grounds, to intervene." Kirkwood calls for "an international code on intervention for wildlife welfare to provide guidance on ethics, methods and standards."

The plight of African wild dogs

One of the most visible and disputed examples of the possible effects of human interference with wild populations concerns the plight of African wild dogs (Woodroffe et al. 1997), distinctive for their large ears and their fur mottled with white, tan, brown, and black patches. Numerous scientists have been trying to figure out whether humans are the cause of the extreme decline of populations of these splendid animals. However, the reasons are not all that clear; the decline could be due to several different factors, not all of them caused by people.

Interference into the lives of wild dogs included vaccinating them against rabies and canine distemper. Some scientists feel that handling and inoculating the dogs were directly responsible for their decline, because the handling weakens their immune system, making them less resistant to stress. Other scientists conclude just the opposite, using the same data. Here we have a very useful example of bright and interested scientists, all of whom care deeply about African wild dogs, not being able to figure out what caused the decline of these animals. What should the researchers do—interfere and possibly cause animals to die from human contact, or let nature take its course? If the rabies and distemper were introduced by domestic dogs, who would not have been there in the absence of people, are we more obligated to try to help the wild dogs than we would be if the rabies and distemper were natural?

Thought experiment: Human interference

The question of when humans should interfere in animals' lives is a difficult one. We must remind ourselves that just because we *can* do something doesn't mean we *should* or *have to* do it. Here are just a few examples of the many possible situations where we might want to think deeply about the ways in which we interfere in animals' lives and consider which of them are justifiable and which are not.

- Should people swim with dolphins, if both the swimmers and the dolphins enjoy it? What if only the humans benefit from the experience? If only the dolphins benefit?

- Is it allowable to use motorboats where dolphins live?

- Should music be played to dolphins through underwater speakers (as has been done as part of some dolphin "tours" packaged for human enjoyment)?

- Is it all right to do "playback studies" in which we record the barks and howls of coyotes and then play them back, fooling individual coyotes into thinking that there are more coyotes in the neighborhood than there really are?

- Is it all right to place colored bands on birds' legs, in order to identify them while we conduct a study of their social behavior, even though the color confuses the birds' natural behavior in selecting mates?

- Should we interfere if we see a predatory animal about to attack its prey, in order to protect the prey? For example, should we try to stop a fox from killing a squirrel? What if the fox is about to attack a stray cat? Should we prevent a companion cat from hunting wild birds?

- In 2007, conservationists in Nepal created a special feeding center where they offer safe food to vultures, whose existence is being threatened because they eat the carcasses of cattle treated with a medication that is toxic to the birds. Do you think this is a good idea? Should we provide food for wild animals whose food supply has been contaminated as a result of human actions?

Deciding on complex questions

When people try to decide what we *should* do by comparing human interventions with what happens naturally in the wild, the conclusions they reach can be troubling. I fear they often end up doing things that harm animals, justifying this by the assumption that anything people do is automatically better than the cruelty of nature. Do we really want an ethic that permits any treatment of animals by humans as long as it is better than what nature typically has in store for similar individuals? I do not think so, because it would allow too many unacceptable practices, such as harming and killing individuals. For example, wolves and other predators have to kill prey animals for food, but this does not give us the freedom or right to kill individual prey.

Another important and related question is whether the pain caused to animals by humans is less than or equal to what animals would experience in the wild. If so, is it then all right to inflict the pain? For many animals, it is difficult to know whether human-caused pain is less than or equal to what the animal would experience in the wild, for we do not know how most individual animals in nature experience pain. We must be careful that using nature's supposed cruelty is not just an excuse for people treating animals in hurtful ways for their own human-centered purposes.

Clearly, it is not possible to settle all these questions on the basis of science alone. That's where common sense comes in. We have to make the best assumptions we can. Thus, even though animals' perceptual world is different from ours, and we can't know for sure what they feel, it seems reasonable to err on the side of assuming that every creature wants to live its life happily, just as we do: eating, resting, finding a mate, playing, learning, enjoying themselves without too much struggle and pain. Consider what Michael Tobias and Jane Morrison (2006) write about donkeys: "What we believe *Equus asinus* most prefers is simply to be left alone so that they may graze casually, marvel at their surroundings, meditate on other life forms, drink plenty of water, have fun, sing, sleep, make love, raise their young, have parties, and discuss the great issues of life."

Our human capacities for empathy and love—which through evolution we have inherited from our animal kin—also come into play when we take a stand to defend the rights of animals to have the best life they can, without undue interference from us.

10

Alternatives to Eating Animals

The suffering of animals we use for food

We generally accept that it's natural for carnivorous wild animals to kill other animals in order to live. But people don't often think (or even know) about the extraordinary and unnatural suffering that humans inflict on the animals that we freely harvest for food, with the help of modern high technology and the animal food sciences. We could name hundreds of ways in which humans use animals for food, from the lunchtime hamburger, Sunday roast chicken, and holiday ham to the hidden ingredients in various products, like gelatin (made from cows' hooves) in vitamin capsules and fruit desserts, or lard (animal fat) used in cookies, pies, and crackers. Even honey taken from bees may be considered an animal food.

Consider that icon of the American breakfast table: the milk poured into a child's glass or breakfast cereal. We are "drinking pain," as one of my colleagues who works in the food industry laments. In our country, milk comes from cows (other countries consume the milk of other animals, like goats, sheep, water buffaloes, and camels). About 5 million dairy cows are kept in confinement in the United States. Female dairy cows are forced to have a calf every year and are milked during seven of their nine months of pregnancy. This is extremely demanding on their bodies and on their psychological states. Their calves are removed from them immediately after birth, so they do not get to drink their own mother's milk. These dairy cows are literally milk machines, and they are not allowed to be mothers, to care for the young whom they have brought into the world. The babies are also deprived of their mothers' nurturing. These calves, who were bred by humans so that their mothers would keep producing more milk for the dairy industry, end up being slaughtered to produce the luxury meat called veal (which we will further discuss below).

Most Americans believe that a meal without animal flesh is incomplete. Each year millions of animals are bred, transported, and housed in slaughterhouses waiting to be killed (and often witnessing other animals being brutally slaughtered). In 1998, in the United States alone, over 26.8 billion animals were killed for food; that translates to about 73,424,657 animals per day, 3,059,361 animals per hour, 50,989 animals per minute, and 850 animals per second.

Numerous animals also die before they reach the slaughterhouses. It has been estimated that more than 780 million chickens, 116 million turkeys, 1.8 million cattle, 2.8 million veal calves, 15.1 million pigs, and 1.2 million sheep die before arriving at U.S. slaughterhouses.[1]

Poultry and eggs are now the most abundant and least expensive animal food products, because of the development of a large-scale industry devoted to their production. Birds are

---

1. *The Farm Report*, Spring 1997.

crammed into tiny, barren wire "battery cages" and cannot perform natural behaviors such as grooming their feathers by "dust bathing," perching, and nesting. Many birds also have their beaks trimmed to keep birds from harming or killing one another, since crowding and inadequate nutrition contribute to behavior such as pulling out each other's feathers and cannibalism. About one-half of the beak is amputated by using a hot cauterizing blade or a precision blade. The pain associated with beak-trimming is intense and long-lasting. Further, caged birds often develop osteoporosis (weakened bones) because of lack of exercise combined with calcium deficiency associated with their forced high rate of egg-laying. Up to about 25% of hens sustain broken bones when they are removed from their cages to be transported to a processing plant. Hens now lay up to 300 eggs per year, almost twice the figure of 170 in 1925.

Food animals may suffer physical and emotional pain not just at the time of slaughter but throughout their lives, often made worse by methods used to turn them into "better food." Individuals are fattened up for human enjoyment by giving them hormones and keeping them in restricted housing where they cannot exercise. Chickens used for meat consumption, or "broilers," now rapidly grow to market weight in about six rather than sixteen weeks. Many individuals die from stress and disease before being slaughtered. Often, fully conscious chickens and turkeys are shocked, drowned in an electrified bath of water, and scalded as they are being prepared for market. Pigs and cattle are supposed to be stunned before being hung upside down by their hind legs, having their throats slit, and bleeding to death, but often they are awake during the whole process. As you are no doubt experiencing, it is shocking and distressing to read about (let alone see) some of these practices that bring to the table the foods Americans take for granted every day.

There also are genetic engineering programs designed to produce bigger and more meaty animals. There is as little regard for the rights of these "bigger and better" animals as there is for their "normal" relatives. Dairy cows stimulated with bovine growth hormone (rBGH) can produce as much as 100 pounds of milk a day, about ten times more than they would normally yield. They suffer from udder infections and are treated with antibiotics as they continue to be exploited for milk. The antibiotics can be transferred to their milk and consumed by people.

Cows, grain, and human starvation

Earlier in this book, we talked about weighing the costs and benefits of using animals. When we look at the costs of eating animals, we see some immediate problems, including the suffering of animals and the dangers to humans who are eating animals treated with chemicals. But in considering costs, we also have to look beyond, to related issues. The way we currently raise animals for food has economic consequences that are not good for human society.

It requires a lot of feed (chiefly plants like grains) to maintain the animals who will eventually become our food. It also requires a lot of land to keep the animals (especially large grazing animals such as beef and dairy cows) and to grow the grain that is used to feed them. For example, it takes eight or nine cattle a year to provide meat for *one* average meat eater. Each cow needs one acre of green plants, corn, or soybeans a year for its feed. Thus, it takes about nine acres of farmland a year to produce the meat that one person eats.

By comparison, a person who does not eat meat can be supported by only half an acre necessary to grow plant food for a year. Twenty vegetarians could live for a year on the amount of grains needed to provide meat for just one meat eater! In the United States alone, livestock eat enough grain and soybeans to feed more than a billion people.[2] It takes about 16 pounds of grain to make a pound of beef. A reduction of meat consumption by only 10% would result in about 12 million more tons of grain for human consumption. This additional grain could feed all of the humans across the world who starve to death each year—about 60 million people!

Veal and public opinion

Perhaps the best example of extreme animal abuse for food is veal, a nonessential food that is purely a culinary luxury, made popular by Italian, French, and Austrian cuisines. Veal comes from unweaned calves who are the offspring of dairy cattle. The calves are taken from their mothers and fed with liquid formula (since their mothers' milk is sold for human consumption). Most formula-fed veal calves are imprisoned for their entire short lives (16 to 18 weeks) in tiny crates only 24 inches wide. Their inability to move and exercise prevents the growth of tough muscles and produces meat that is tender. Before they are killed, their iron intake is restricted to below normal levels, making the calves anemic. Anemia, a deficiency of red blood cells, results in a pale or white color of the meat, which is highly valued: the paler the carcass of the slaughtered animal, the higher the grade or quality of the meat and the more money paid to the producer.

---

2. See http://supak.com/organic_gardening/farming.htm, where it is claimed that the number of human beings who could be fed by the grain and soybeans eaten by U.S. livestock is 1.3 billion.

The demand for formula-fed veal has dropped sharply since 1985, and production has now stabilized at approximately 750,000 calves per year[3]—a decrease of over 400%. Public outrage over how veal calves are treated was the major reason for this decline. Clearly, what people think does have an influence, so we must voice our protests against such horrible practices. It is essential to keep up the pressure on the veal industry in order to reduce or eliminate this cause of immense cruelty to animals for the sake of a food that is not needed by anyone.

Hunting and fishing

Hunting and fishing are popular activities. According to a survey (Duda et al. 1996), about 14 million Americans, sixteen years and older, hunt each year, and about 36 million Americans (in the same age group) fish. Most of them are males, but females are increasingly participating in the sport. These enthusiasts often like to hang signs that say "Gone Fishin'" or "Gone Huntin'." But what these slogans really mean is "Gone killing."

While hunters and fishers often eat the animals they kill, a meal is not always the goal. Some people engage in trophy hunting and sport hunting, or trophy fishing and sport fishing, where they kill animals for the thrill of the hunt and to come home with a trophy. Others make a point of not killing; they stalk the animals but do not shoot at them or catch them, or they catch fish and then throw them back into the water. People who catch fish and then throw them back into the

---

3. http://vanguardpublications.blogspot.com/2006_09_03_vanguard publications_archive.html.

water deny that any damage was done to the fish, even though they used a hook to catch their prey.

To satisfy the needs of the sport of fishing, more than 150 species of fish have been introduced into North American waters outside their natural range. Many fish are raised in hatcheries that are essentially zoos, where they are held captive, fed well, and protected until they are released to become prey for humans who fish. The introduction of these species has changed the ecological balance in numerous bodies of water. Introduced species have spread diseases to natural fish populations, or have displaced or preyed on native species. Because of the detrimental effects that introduced fish have on an ecosystem and its inhabitants, a new ethic put forth by conservation groups and fish biologists urges caution when stocking is being considered.

Hunting and fishing involve killing animals with devices (such as guns) for which the animals have not evolved natural defenses. No animal on earth has adequate defense against a human armed with a gun, a bow and arrow, a trap that can maim, a snare that can strangle, or a fishing lure designed for the sole purpose of fooling fish into thinking they have found something good to eat.

The practice of catching fish just for fun and then letting them go is often referred to as "catch and release." Even when fish are caught and released by people who claim they are practicing conservation, the animals are often returned to the wild weak and injured, their mouths torn up by the fish hook. As mentioned in chapter 4, fish are capable of suffering in ways similar to humans and other mammals. The stress responses of fish to stimuli that lead to anxiety and fear closely mimic those of other vertebrates. Furthermore, no one knows how many fish die after being caught and tossed. It is estimated that 5% to 10% of trout die merely from the stress of being handled.

Even if hunters only stalk animals but do not try to kill them, animals suffer during the chase. They are anxious and scared. Patrick Bateson (1997), at the University of Cambridge in England, has shown that red deer hunted by dogs show stress responses similar to symptoms that are seen when animals are frightened. Hunted animals showed high levels of cortisol (a hormone released in the body under stress) from the start of the hunt, and levels were higher in deer hunted for longer distances. The deer's muscles also showed signs of physical damage, and the hunted deer showed extreme signs of fatigue. Non-hunted deer did not show the same stress responses: they had low levels of stress hormones. Clearly, the animals did not like being chased and hunted, and could not know that they wouldn't be killed. Imagine being chased for the sake of being chased, without knowing what will happen to you if and when you are caught.

Vegetarianism: A good alternative

Because of the animal cruelty involved in meat eating, many people choose to reduce or eliminate their consumption of meat. They try gradually cutting back on hamburgers and other animal products—from five to two servings a week for a month, then from two to one for a month, then one for two months, and so on. Not only might you be doing yourself and animals a favor, but by participating in the movement toward vegetarianism, you might also one day help to feed other humans who would otherwise starve to death. Remember that a reduction of meat consumption by only 10% would result in about 12 million more tons of grain for human consumption. This additional grain could feed all of the humans who starve to death each year—about 60 million people.

There are many good reasons to switch to a vegetarian diet, in addition to the benefit to animals. Vegetarian diets are much healthier than diets that contain meat, especially meat that has been injected with various types of hormones or meat from animals who were stressed before they were killed. Colin Campbell and Junshi Chen (1994) made a long-term study of dietary habits in mainland China. The results suggested if people in Western countries adopted a plant-based diet, with fat providing only 10% to 20% of the total calories, they could significantly decrease the occurrence of chronic degenerative diseases such as various cancers and heart disorders. (See also Campbell 2005.)

There are many types of vegetarianism and numerous reasons for becoming a vegetarian. Vegetarians can be classified as follows:

- *lacto-ovo vegetarians,* who eat eggs and dairy products but no meat;
- *lacto-vegetarians,* who eat dairy products but no eggs or meat;
- *ovo-vegetarians,* who eat eggs but no dairy products or meat;
- *vegans,* who consume no animal products at all—meat, dairy products, or eggs—and instead get their protein from legumes and beans, nuts, and soy foods like tofu and tempeh;
- *macrobiotic vegetarians,* who live on whole grains, sea and land vegetables, beans, fermented soy products such as miso, and sometimes small quantities of fish;
- *natural hygienists,* who eat plant foods, combine foods in certain ways, and believe in periodic fasting;
- *raw foodists,* who eat only uncooked nonmeat foods; and

- *fruitarians,* who eat mainly fruits but also nuts, seeds, and certain vegetables.

The philosopher Michael Allen Fox (1999) lists the following as the main arguments for vegetarianism:

1. It promotes good health.
2. It reduces animal suffering and death.
3. It promotes an impartial moral concern for the well-being of both animals and humans.
4. It is a response to concerns such as environmental problems caused by meat production, world hunger, and social injustice.
5. It promotes universal compassion and kinship with other animals.
6. It affirms the values of religious teachings such as nonviolence and the sacredness of nature.

He notes that vegetarianism focuses attention not only on human-animal relationships or humanity's relationship to nature, but also on choosing a way of life that is morally and ecologically preferable.

Now ask yourself what you can do to make life better for animals who are used for food.

- If you eat meat, why do you do so?
- Is it out of habit, because it's what you were fed since childhood?
- Is it because you crave it?
- Do you believe you need it for the protein? Are there other ways you could satisfy your body's protein requirements?

- If you're not able to stop eating animal foods completely, could you cut back on your consumption of meat of all kinds and other animal products?
- Would you talk to other people about the importance of respecting animals and not letting them be killed for food, especially when it is not necessary?

By asking these questions, you can truly make a difference in the lives of many animals.

Stop the killing of great apes for food

Bushmeat—the meat of wild animals killed in their home forests—is a very popular commercial food product in many parts of the world. Chimpanzee and gorilla meat is favored, as is kangaroo meat. About 20% of bushmeat comes from non-human primates—our nearest relatives. Its consumption (even in elegant European restaurants) and trade is the biggest threat to biodiversity in some African forests. In the Congo Basin, bushmeat is the primary source of animal protein for the majority of families.

There simply are not enough chimpanzees or gorillas to sustain their slaughter for food. In one study, it was found that about 800 gorillas were killed each year in the Kika, Moloundou, and Mabale triangle in Cameroon. If only 3,000 gorillas live in that 10,000-square-kilometer area, the taking of this many gorillas simply is not sustainable. About 400 chimpanzees were also killed in this area. Thus, 1,200 great apes in one small area were killed. Anthony Rose of the Bushmeat Project (a program of the Biosynergy Institute in Hermosa Beach, California) notes that this year more than 3,000 gorillas and 4,000 chimpanzees will be illegally butchered. That is five times the number of gorillas on Rwanda's Mount Visoke and twenty times more chimpanzees than live near Tanzania's Gombe Stream, Jane Goodall's study area. More great apes are eaten each year than are now kept in all the zoos and laboratories worldwide. Dale Peterson has written an excellent book on this disturbing topic, *Eating Apes* (2003).

The bushmeat trade is an example of how different human activities that seem to be unrelated actually influence one another greatly. For example, the large increase in the availability of bushmeat is a result of increased logging activities. Logging companies build new roads into areas that previously were very difficult to reach, and they allow hunters to travel on company vehicles to hard-to-reach areas where gorillas, chimpanzees, and other large animals are found. The hunters kill all but the smallest animals and carry meat to logging camps where loggers consume some of it. The remaining meat goes to market in cities. As logging increases, so does the number of individuals who are brutally slaughtered. There now are campaigns to have logging companies stop the transport of bushmeat.

The killing of great apes is illegal in every country in which it takes place, but very few hunters are ever punished. There are international laws concerning the killing of endangered species (for example, chimpanzees), but it is difficult to catch hunters in action. Although people have known about the harmful effects of the bushmeat trade for years, there has not been much interest in this activity until recently. But now, most conservationists realize that if commercial bushmeat hunting continues, there will be devastating effects on the population of chosen animals. Thus, there is a lot interest in stopping the bushmeat trade.

Of course, logging is not only a problem in Africa. Many conservation biologists are supporting programs that limit commercial logging in numerous countries so that habitat and animals can be protected. One way to decrease the need for wood is to be careful when you buy wood products and ask questions about the source of the timber. When you go to buy something made of wood, ask where the wood came from. If you are unsure about its origins, find out more. It is possible that the wood that you are buying in some way contributed to the death of great apes and other animals who became easy to find and kill because roads were built for other reasons. The Rescued Wood Bowl Company in Fort Collins, Colorado, is setting an example by using only rescued and recycled wood that was on the way to a landfill.[4]

There is also a move in the music world by the Gibson Guitar Company to use what is called "smartwood" to replace wood from dwindling rain forests that is used to make guitars. Who would have ever thought that playing music with a guitar may be directly related to killing animals, not to mention killing lovely trees and decimating fragile habitats? Who would ever have thought that playing music could be associated with harming faraway rain forests or be linked to brutally killing animals?

Although many of us live far away from places where bushmeat is slaughtered and consumed, we can protest this illegal activity by being careful about what we buy and by expressing our outrage about this carnage. Each of us counts, and we all can make a difference if we act.[5]

---

4. For more about rescued wood, see www.harrywicks.com/about .html.
5. See http://bushmeat.net and http://biosynergy.org.

11

Poisons, Eye Shadow, and Fur

*Using Animals for Product Testing
and Clothing*

C ruelty to animals takes many forms. The use of animals'
bodies to provide fur for clothing and accessories is one
example that has received much publicity. But let's start with
the less visible practice of subjecting animals to scientific research in the laboratory, with the aim of ensuring the safe use
of products ranging from cosmetics to various chemicals and
medications. Clearly, this kind of testing is cruel to animals,
causing them unnecessary pain, injury, and usually death by
the end of the study. But is it really necessary for the human
benefits that are sought, and are there no alternatives?

Millions of individual animals—including dogs, cats, rats,
mice, guinea pigs, and rabbits—are used for testing cosmetics
such as deodorants, shampoos, soaps, and eye makeup.[1] When
we weigh the costs and benefits of such testing, we have to acknowledge that these products are nonessential, compared with
drugs that treat illness, for example. And yet, even though such
animal tests are not required by law, many cosmetic companies

---

1. See Animalearn Fact Files, Product Testing.

continue to conduct them. Neither the U.S. Food and Drug Administration (FDA) nor the Consumer Product Safety Commission requires that animals be used to test the safety of products for humans.

Lethal-dose tests

Lethal-dose (LD) tests are an attempt to measure the toxicity or potential harmfulness of products such as cosmetics or drugs by forcing live animals to ingest the substance to be tested. Animals receive a single dose of the substance either in their mouth, by a stomach tube, by inhaling a vapor powder or spray, by having it applied to the skin, or intravenously. The dose at which 50% of the animals die is called the lethal-dose 50, or LD50, and that at which 100% die is called the LD100. Many animals become sick and suffer greatly from convulsions, seizures, muscle cramps, abdominal pain, paralysis, and bleeding from the ears, eyes, nose, and rectum. If fewer than 50% of the animals die, the tests need to be repeated with a different amount of the substance in order to yield the LD50. Thus, the suffering of animals is increased.

The cruelty of these tests is of course a major objection to them. In addition, they have been criticized as being ineffective and invalid. The results are only specific to the conditions in which they were used, so they cannot be generalized from species to species. In other words, knowing how a chemical affects laboratory rats does not necessarily tell you how that chemical will affect animals of another species, such as dogs, parakeets, or humans. Sometimes the findings cannot even be generalized by gender, so that if the product was tested on male animals, the results might not apply to females of the same species.

The LD50 often is used to estimate the safe dose of a product for humans. For example, paraquat was introduced in 1960 as an herbicide, a poison that protects crops by killing weeds harmful to them, and the lethal dose test was used to determine the health risks of exposing humans to it. Because the LD50 for rats was 120 milligrams per kilogram of body weight, it was thought that humans exposed to fewer milligrams of paraquat would be safe. However, in twelve years, more than 400 humans died from exposure to this chemical, and it was estimated that the LD50 was much smaller, about 4 milligrams per kilogram of body weight.

Animal tests are not the litmus test for safety. Shockingly, more than 100,000 people a year die from side effects of animal-tested drugs—yet drugs and chemicals are still approved as "safe" based on animal testing. On the positive side, the Diabetes Research Institute announced in February 2006 that it would no longer conduct experiments on mice. Scientists from the Institute had concluded that the composition of insulin-producing islet cells in the human pancreas is so different from that of rodents that tests using rodents are no longer relevant for human studies.

Rabbits and the Draize Test for eye irritation

Since the 1940s, rabbits have been the victims of a cosmetic testing method known as the Draize Test, used to determine whether products would irritate sensitive tissue such as the eyes. In the test, a liquid or solid substance is placed in one eye of each of several rabbits. Changes in the cornea, conjunctiva, and iris are then observed and scored. The rabbits' eyes are inspected at 24, 48, and 72 hours after application of the substance, and again at 4 and 7 days. Both injury and potential for recovery are noted.

The Draize Test is a horrible test, and the animals suffer immensely. Consumer protests against widespread use of the Draize Test led to the development of non-animal alternatives to many types of animal testing. The Coalition to Abolish the Draize Test—formed in 1979 by Henry Spira, founder of Animal Rights International—eventually achieved radical changes in product-safety testing worldwide.[2] Spira's campaign unleashed a growing movement against causing animals discomfort. By 1981 the cosmetics industry awarded $1 million to Johns Hopkins School of Hygiene and Public Health to establish the Center for Alternatives to Animal Testing (CAAT).

Testing environmental pollutants

Animals are also used in toxicology research, the study of the effects on living things of environmental pollutants. The toxic substances studied include poisons that cause cancer (carcinogens), birth defects, and numerous other diseases. Some of these poisons are present in household or industrial products. Examples include trichloroethylene (TCE), used in spices, general anesthetics, and decaffeinated coffee; the pesticides lindane and DDT (dichloro-diphenyl-trichloro-ethane); and DES, a chemical that promotes growth in cattle and poultry.

The devastating effect of DDT on wildlife and the environment was first described in a famous book published in 1962,

---

2. Spira's amazing accomplishments in the field of animal protection are well documented in Peter Singer's book *Ethics into Action: Henry Spira and the Animal Rights Movement* (1998).

Silent Spring by the biologist Rachel Carson. Carson anguished over the mass deaths of songbirds due to extensive government spraying with DDT; the resulting eerie silence at feeding stations and springs inspired the title of her book. By publicizing the effects of dangerous chemicals on all forms of animals and plant life, she influenced the growth of the environmental movement and helped reform pesticide use in the United States.

Since we know how damaging environmental poisons are to wildlife, are we justified in deliberately exposing animals to such poisons in the laboratory? Even though the intention is to ensure safety for humans, in many cases the data from animals simply do not apply to humans in any direct way, and often the methods that are used are not adequate to draw meaningful conclusions about how pollutants affect humans. Numerous technical and scientific problems arise when we try to use animals to make predictions about human responses to drugs and environmental chemicals. Many of these problems are related to the lack of progress science has made in helping humans deal with the negative effects of environmental poisons.

A good place to start reading in this area is Alix Fano's book, *Lethal Laws: Animal Testing, Human Health and Environmental Policy* (1997). Fano reviews available data in the field of toxicology testing, shows why animal models rarely if ever work, and then suggests numerous non-animal alternatives that produce more reliable results. Some noninvasive non-animal alternatives include the use of human cell cultures, human living tissues, computer-based models, and human volunteer studies. Some prestigious scientists agree with Fano's argument that the use of animals to test poisons is outdated and no longer useful, because scientists now know the limitations of animal experiments as a way of predicting human results. She quotes Philip Abelson, a famous American scientist and former editor of *Science,* a very prestigious scientific publication, as saying: "The standard carcinogen tests that use rodents are an obsolescent relic of the ignorance of past decades." These tests do not work and should be stopped.

Among the major criticisms of these tests are the facts that excessively large doses of poisons are given to the animals and the chemicals are often administered in ways that do not mimic the human experience. For instance, in some studies hair dyes were fed to animals instead of being applied to their fur or skin. Fano also points out that even though some animal tests show clear evidence of the negative effects of chemicals on the animals, the results have been ignored and the chemical industry has actually grown rather than been slowed down.

Animals used for fur

How animals are used to manufacture clothes made of fur continues to be of interest to numerous animal protection groups worldwide. Wild fur-bearing animals, over 40 million individuals, including various species of foxes, mink, and sable, are cruelly maimed and killed for profit.[3] Many are trapped using various types of contraptions that cause enormous psychological and physical suffering. These devices include leg-hold traps, wire snares that encircle an animal and pull tighter as the animal struggles, and conibear traps that grip the entire body and break the neck or back. Beavers are often trapped in water and drown after struggling for some time. Often companion dogs are trapped when traps are set to capture other species. There are no laws in the United States regarding how trapped animals may or may not be killed.

---

3. See Animalearn Fact Files, Fur, #8.

Some animals, such as mink, are "ranched-raised" (raised on farms) for the express purpose of being slaughtered for use in coats and other items of clothing. Recently, even dogs and cats (either captured strays or individuals bred specifically for use as clothing) have been used to make fur products (sometimes deceptively sold as "faux fur," which means "false fur"). These individuals typically are kept in deplorable conditions before being killed by being beaten, hanged, suffocated, bled to death, or skinned alive. In the United States, using dog or cat fur is illegal, but there are no federal laws prohibiting the import of such fur produced abroad. In 2007 legislation was introduced requiring labeling on every fur garment and banning the import and sale of fur from raccoon dogs, which live in Asian and northern European forests, as well as domestic dogs.

There also are no laws in the United States that regulate fur farms, although countries such as England, Scotland, and Wales have outlawed fur farming on the basis of "public morality."[4] Needless to say, farmed animals endure all the suffering of captive animals in zoos. However, farmed animals are killed and are not even able live out their lives in cages. The fur industry has a set of guidelines, but following them is voluntary, and there is no monitoring of fur farms. Animals such as mink are killed by neck-snapping ("popping"). They show great distress when removed from their cages to be killed—screeching, losing control of bladder and bowels, fighting for their lives. Gassing is also used, as are lethal injections, both of which cause pain and prolonged suffering before animals are released by death. The carcasses of some farmed animals are even sold for dissection, so there is a connection between raising animals

---

4. www.infurmation.com/pdf/linzey02.pdf.

for fur and their use in education. Supporting the practice of dissection of animals in the classroom can also mean supporting the fur industry.

What can you do?

There are many things you can do if you are concerned about the plight of animals who are used for testing and clothing. Buy cruelty-free products that are not tested on animals. There are numerous cruelty-free products available. (You can get this information from reading labels and searching the Worldwide Web; using the phrase "cruelty-free products" yields numerous sites including the ones listed in the Resources section, under "Organizations and Web Sites.") Buying stock in companies that practice cruelty-free testing of their products can help to encourage this trend in the industry. You can choose to buy shoes, belts, and bags that are not made of leather, and products that are plant- rather than animal-based, like organic cotton and hemp. Boycott stores that sell fur. Refuse to dissect animals at school (see the next chapter for more on this topic).

Campaigns against fur-wearing have resulted in large declines in fur sales in the last decade, but many people still continue to wear fur and leather products. The lives of animals have been saved by people going to the mass media and reaching millions of concerned consumers about the horrible treatment to which animals are subjected in the clothing industry. Nonetheless, much more needs to be done. Educate others. By setting an example yourself and by talking to others, you can truly help numerous other animals who cannot speak out for themselves.

Other animal models that do not work: Social deprivation and eating disorders

Many observers now believe that studies based on animal models yield little knowledge useful to humans, despite enormous investments of time and money, and the sacrifice of animals' lives.[5] In the behavioral sciences, two examples of the inadequacy of animal models are the use of maternal and social deprivation (depriving young animals of mothering and other social contact) to learn about human depression, and the use of animals to study human eating disorders, including obesity, anorexia, and bulimia.

Following the deplorable work of Harry Harlow (1959) at the University of Wisconsin, socially deprived monkeys are commonly used to study psychological and physiological aspects of depression. Martin Stephens (1986) has published a valuable criticism of this work, as has the Animal Protection Institute. Individuals typically are removed from their mothers and other family members soon after birth and raised alone, often in small, dark, barren cages called "depression pits." In their impoverished prisons, isolated monkeys scream in despair, become self-destructive, and eventually withdraw from the world. The only social contacts with these unsocialized, frightened, and distraught monkeys occur when blood is drawn or other physiological measures are taken, or when they are introduced to other monkeys, whom they avoid or who maim or occasionally kill them.

Besides the fact that these types of studies are ethically repulsive, numerous flaws plague deprivation studies, including

---

5. See Animalearn Fact Files, Animal Experiments, #3, and *Sacred Cows and Golden Geese* (Greek & Greek 2000).

the lack of human clinical relevance. Researchers view human depression as a distinctly human condition. Simplistic animal models of human depression do not work for the diagnosis, treatment, or prevention of human depression. Nonetheless, federal agencies heavily fund (with taxpayers' money) these studies in which baby monkeys are torn from their mothers and made to suffer panic attacks, anxiety, and depression. Even people who accept other forms of animal research are offended by the horrors of deprivation research. Many in the public believe it should be stopped immediately. No ends justify the means.

Kenneth Shapiro (1998) has written extensively about the use of animal models in psychological research, specifically in eating disorders. Despite research in which animals are starved, force-fed, or subjected to binge-purge cycles, Shapiro found that only 37% of clinicians who treat people for eating disorders even knew about the results of such research. Of those who did know about the research, 87% said animal models were not used to design human treatment programs. The success rate of animal models for application in human clinical practice is extremely low. You probably would not even go to the movies if you had the same slim chance of arriving successfully.

Animal studies are often conducted merely because that's how research was conducted in the past and it's convenient to continue the same procedures. Neither of these "reasons" can adequately justify the cruelty of such research, even in areas where human health needs are at stake, as in biomedical and toxicological research. Unfortunately, the use of animal models often creates false hopes for humans in need. It is estimated that only 1% to 3.5% of the decline in the rate of human mortality since 1900 has stemmed from animal research. The prestigious *New England Journal of Medicine* has called the "war on cancer" a qualified failure. And more than 100,000 people die annually from the side effects of animal-tested drugs.

Some biomedical models have been seriously misleading. For example, early monkey models of polio used by the pathologist Simon Flexner yielded flawed data concerning the mechanism of infection (Medical Research Modernization Committee 1998). Flexner concluded that polio only infected the nervous systems of monkeys, not those of humans. However, research using human tissue showed that the polio virus could be cultivated on tissue that was not from the nervous system. In another example of misleading research, chimpanzees were used to study AIDS, but they do not naturally contract AIDS. When a disease is artificially induced in an animal, the course of the disease is different from a naturally occurring infection in humans. Therefore, the conclusions drawn from such biomedical models are not accurate, and as a result many humans die.

Non-animal alternatives need to be developed and used to learn about human behavioral and other medical problems. These alternatives may include human studies, even though they are more time-consuming, expensive, risky, and difficult to defend ethically than animal studies. However, the benefits of all alternatives will flow not only to numerous human beings, but also to countless innocent nonhumans—our animal kin.

The effects of field-workers on animals

We have indicated a few of the many ethical concerns about studies of captive animals in the laboratory. In addition, there are ethical issues associated with the study of animals in the wild. The presence of researchers in the midst of an animal's habitat is itself a form of interference into their lives: "just being there" and walking around can have significant impacts on wild animals. Nonetheless, field studies contribute information on the complexity and richness of animal lives that is very useful to those interested in animal well-being. Students of behavior often want to be able to identify individuals, assign gender and age, follow individuals as they move about, or record various physiological measurements including heart rate and body temperature. Animals living under field conditions are generally more difficult to study than individuals living in more confined conditions, and various methods (e.g., trapping, marking, fitting with telemetric devices) are often used to make them more accessible. The use of leg-hold traps results in serious injuries to animals, including swelling of limbs, lacerations, fractures, and amputation.

I have long been concerned with how various methods of study can influence the animals being studied—for example, their nesting and reproductive behaviors, dominance relationships, mate choice, use of space, vulnerability to predators, and feeding and care-giving behaviors. Models that are generated from these studies can be misleading because of human intrusions that *appear* to be neutral but that really do have an effect. We need to be sure that the behavior patterns that are being studied and analyzed truly are a reliable indicator of an individual's normal behavior when taking into account his or her age, gender, and social status. If the information used to make assessments of an animal's well-being is unreliable, then it follows that the conclusions that are reached and the animal models that are generated are also unreliable and can mislead current and future research programs. And, of course, our errors can have horrible consequences for the lives of the animals being studied. Our research ethic—the principles governing the way we conduct research—should require that we learn about the normal behavior of animals (as well as natural variations of their behavior patterns). In that way, we will understand better just how we are affecting the animals when we study them in the field. The studies that I discuss now show just how we do affect the behavior and lives of various animals when we intrude into their lives, and this information can be used as future studies are designed. Of course, it might just be that we influence animals in ways unknown to us, but if we know about the normal behavior of individuals of a given species or of closely related species, we can use this information to halt research practices that have a negative impact on the individuals we are studying.

Here are some representative studies to show how widespread are researcher influences, and the diversity of species that are affected.

A study of the habitat preferences of large grey mongooses involved capturing them, fitting them with tracking devices, and then recapturing them to collect the data. These methods actually influenced the very behaviors that were being tracked—the animals' use of space. Even minor effects need to be considered in research projects involving such practices. It is important to ask whether the movement patterns we observe in a wild animal are natural movements typical of the species, or are they the movements of individuals trying to avoid traps or human observers. Suppose, for example, that data are being collected about animals' movement patterns in order to design appropriate enclosures for them. If the enclosures are going to meet the animals' actual needs for space and other habitat preferences, then clearly the data used to make design decisions must be based on reliable, accurate observations. Magpies, large and very intelligent birds, who are not used to being around people, spend so much time avoiding humans that this takes time away from essential activities such as feeding. Researchers interested in gathering data on feeding patterns by these birds would have to be sure that their own presence did not change the typical feeding patterns of the species.

Adélie penguins exposed to aircraft and directly to humans showed profound changes in behavior, including deviation from a direct course back to a nest and increased abandonment of the young in the nest. Overall effects due to exposure to aircraft that prevented foraging penguins from returning their nests included a decrease of 15% in the number of birds in a colony and an active nest mortality (death of chicks) of 8%. There are also large increases in penguins' heart rates. Here, models concerning reproductive success and parental investment (the amount of time and energy they put into their young) would be misleading, once again because of the methods used.

Trumpeter swans do not show such adverse effects to aircraft. However, the noise and visible presence of stopped vehicles produces changes in incubation behavior by trumpeter females that could result in decreased productivity due to increases in the mortality of eggs and hatchlings. Once again, data on the reproductive behavior of these birds would be misleading.

The foraging behavior of Little penguins (average weight 1,100 grams, or less than 2.5 pounds) is influenced by their carrying a small device (weighing about 60 grams) that measures the speed and depth of their dives. The small attachments result in decreased foraging efficiency as they dive for food. However, when female spotted hyenas wear radio collars weighing less than 2% of their body weight, there seems to be little effect on their behavior. Similar results have been found for small rodents: small radio collars do not affect their movements in a way that would increase their risk of being caught by predatory birds. Changes in behavior such as these, caused by the equipment or techniques used in the study, are called the *instrument effect*.

Placing a tag on the wings of ruddy ducks leads to decreased rates of courtship (the number of times an hour a bird engaged in courting behavior) and more time sleeping and preening. In this case, data on activity rhythms and maintenance behaviors such as preening would have been misleading.

When zebra finches are tagged with a leg band, the color of the band influences the birds' choice of mates. Females with black bands and males with red bands had higher reproductive success than birds with other colors. Blue and green bands were especially unattractive to both females and males.

The weight of radio collars can influence dominance relationships in adult female meadow voles. When voles wear a collar that is greater than 10% of their live body mass, there is a significant loss of dominance in relation to other females and males. When researchers are unaware of the effects of the tracking device (the collar) on the behavior they are tracking (relationships among female voles), erroneous data are generated, so that the results of the study are unreliable.

Methods of trapping can also lead to misleading results. Trapping methods can bias age ratios and sex ratios in some species of birds. Mist nets captured a higher proportion of juveniles, whereas traps captured more adults. Furthermore, dominant males tended to monopolize traps that were baited with food, leading to erroneous data on sex ratios. These are extremely important results because age and sex ratios are important data for many different researchers interested in behavior, behavioral ecology, and population biology.

Not only do research methods influence a wide variety of behavior patterns, but they can also influence susceptibility to infection. Ear-tagging white-footed mice leads to higher infestations by larval ticks because the tag gets in the way when the mouse tries to clean its ears. Thus, for researchers interested in grooming behavior, the presence of ear tags could influence results. These examples suffice to show that animal models that do not take into account researcher effects can provide erroneous information about the behavior of numerous and diverse species. And, if this misinformation is used to design future studies, build housing for captive animals, or evaluate well-being, then erroneous conclusions will be drawn. Some of the problems are serious enough to warrant the abandonment of animal models of human disease or behavior. In situations where models are not being developed, some of the problems warrant the development of more reliable and more humane methods. In addition, there are costs in terms of the interference into the animal's life, perhaps to the detriment of successful mating, feeding, and other essential tasks, not to mention its discomfort.

Taking precautions

While researchers often cannot know about various aspects of animal behavior before we arrive in the field, our presence does seem to influence what animals do when we enter into their worlds. What appear to be relatively small changes at the individual level can have wide-ranging effects in both the short and long term. On-the-spot decisions often need to be made, and knowledge of what these changes will mean to the lives of the animals who are involved demands serious attention. A guiding principle should be that the wild animals we are privileged to study should be respected, and when we are unsure about how our activities will influence their lives, we should err in favor of the animals and not engage in these practices until we know the consequences of our acts. This precautionary principle will serve us and the animals well.

The consideration of important ethical questions can be enriching, helping us to discover new ways of interacting with animals, possibilities that benefit the animals as well as ourselves. There is a continuing need to develop and improve general guidelines for research on free-living and captive animals. Professional societies can play a large role in the generation of guidelines, and many professional journals now require that contributors provide a statement saying that the research they conducted was performed in agreement with accepted regulations. Guidelines should be progressive as well as regulatory, bringing improvements and new alternatives to existing practices. We should not be satisfied that things are better now than they were in the "bad old days," and we should work for a future in which even these enlightened times will be viewed as the bad old days for animals.

Much progress has already been made in the development of guidelines, and the challenge is to make them more binding, effective, and specific. Jane Goodall and I established a group called Ethologists for the Ethical Treatment of Animals to help enforce the highest of ethical standards in behavioral research. If possible, we should also work for consistency among countries that share common attitudes toward animal protection; research in some countries (including the United States) is less regulated in favor of animals than research in other countries (such as those in the European Union). Researchers who are exposed to the pertinent issues, and who think about them and engage in open and serious debate, can then carry these lessons into their research projects and impart this knowledge to colleagues and students. Not knowing all of the subtleties of philosophical arguments—details over which even professional ethicists disagree—should not be a stumbling block or an insurmountable barrier to learning.

12

Dissection and Vivisection

*We Don't Need to Cut Animals
to Learn about Life*

*The Three R's:
Reduction, refinement, and replacement*

Because of the growing movement to end cruelty to animals, there is increasing pressure to develop non-animal alternatives to the use of animals in research and education. The idea of the Three R's—reduction, refinement, and replacement of laboratory animal use—was introduced in *The Principles of Humane Experimental Technique* (1959), written by two British scientists, William M. S. Russell and Rex Burch. This was the first book to present in a clear fashion how animals could be protected from human abuse. A handful of researchers adopted the Three R's soon after the book was published, and over time the principles gradually gained acceptance. Today many researchers use them to organize their research projects to make them more humane.

Reduction alternatives use fewer animals to obtain the same amount of data or allow more information to be obtained from a given number of animals. The goal of reduction is to decrease the total number of animals that must be used.

Refinement alternatives lessen animals' pain and distress. When developing refinement alternatives it is appropriate to assume that if a procedure is painful to humans, it will also be painful to animals. Refinement alternatives include the use of analgesics and/or anesthetics to alleviate any potential pain. Environmental enrichment is also a type of refinement. Examples of enrichment are items that reduce boredom for laboratory animals: a running wheel that provides exercise; objects that can be manipulated, like toys or even hair rollers; or games that can be played on a computer. Another form of enrichment is to hide food or give the animals frozen food, so that they have to work to get their meal, which is closer to the way they feed in the wild.

Replacement alternatives are methods that do not use live animals. One example is "in vitro" systems. *In vitro* is a Latin term literally meaning "in glass"; it can also refer to other artificial environments outside a living body of a plant or animal. For example, living material may be cultured in small dishes called petri dishes or in test tubes. In vitro studies can often replace in vivo ("in a living body") studies, which make use of living animals. Mathematical and computer models also can be used to replace animal studies.

Are dissection and vivisection all they are cut out to be?

In order to study animals, do we always have to *dissect* (cut apart) dead animals or *vivisect* living ones? Opinions vary on this question. Some teachers and researchers argue that dissection and vivisection are necessary because they are the only way in which students can learn about physiology and anatomy. They claim that non-animal alternatives are not as useful educationally, whereas other teachers and researchers maintain that non-animal alternatives are as good as or better than either dissection or vivisection. Members of about 170 species, including at least 10 million vertebrates, are used annually for various levels of education in the United States. It has been estimated that about 90% of the animals used for dissection, including frogs, turtles, and fish, are caught in the wild, and this can have an impact on natural populations, especially for those species in which there are few wild individuals remaining. The philosopher Steven Sapontzis (1995) points out that killing and dissecting can teach students unethical attitudes about animals, leading them to think that animals are weak because they can be easily dominated by humans, that exploitation of the weak by the strong is all right. These practices can also make teachers and students become desensitized to the plight of other animals and lose respect for the animals being used.[1]

Many educational institutions, ranging from middle schools to colleges, universities (undergraduate and graduate programs) to professional programs, require students to cut apart or dissect specimens that have been prepared for this purpose, or to do experiments on live animals, to vivisect them. Many students do not say anything to teachers about their objections to dissection or vivisection, and many students do not know that numerous non-animal alternatives options are readily available.[2]

---

1. See Animalearn, Fact Files, Animals in Education, #1, and Animal Experiments, #3.
2. For more information on alternatives, see www.aavs.org, www.idausa .org/campaigns/dissection/undergradscience.html, and www.petakids .com/disindex.html.

They are not told in school about alternatives unless they ask about them. For example, Jonathan Balcombe, Associate Director for Education at the Humane Society of United States, noted that in 1995, all twenty-four county school systems in Maryland permitted students to use alternatives to dissection, but only one county had a written policy that required students and/or parents to be notified of this option. Why would students refrain from voicing their objections to these practices? Embarrassment, ridicule by peers, and perhaps feeling that the only recourse would be to change their career choice may make students decide to do things to animals that they do not want to do.

Supporters of dissection frequently argue that dissection or vivisection is a "hands on" experience essential to the student's education. Some biologists think that if someone does not want to cut animals up, they should not study biology. These scientists overlook that fact that there are many different types of biology, and not all types would require examining animal specimens in this way. For example, anatomical or physiological studies may require it, but ethology, the study of animal behavior, involves watching animals behave and would not necessitate dissection.

There is no evidence for the claim that hands-on dissection or vivisection experience is essential to a student's education. Many teachers who use dissection and vivisection in their classrooms do so despite the fact that they do not know whether exercises such as these actually are effective teaching methods. Appeals to "history"—saying that this is the way we have always taught biology—are weak arguments for practices that either should never have been freely implemented in the first place, or are simply outdated because of advances in other fields.

For example, in its position statement on animal use, the

Human Anatomy and Physiology Society (HAPS), states that "dissection and the manipulation of animal tissues and organs are essential elements in scientific investigation and introduce students to the excitement and challenge of future careers." While there is no doubt that dissection, vivisection, and experimentation have played major roles in many courses in the past, it is not at all clear that these activities are "essential" in the sense that science could not be carried on without them, particularly with all of today's technological advances. Furthermore, HAPS's view is not necessarily consistent with the nature of scientific inquiry as practiced today. There are many different types of inquiry that can be labeled "scientific," and there seems to be more open-mindedness now among practicing scientists. Certainly, it would undermine educating future scientists if they were taught that there was only *one* way to teach science, including anatomy and physiology. Furthermore, calling dissection and vivisection "essential elements in scientific investigation" is misleading, for most scientific endeavors, broadly defined, do not involve these practices.

A large number of U.S. medical schools do not currently use live animals in their regular medical curricula, and of those 126 that do, all but one offer alternative exercises for students who do not want to participate directly in procedures that use live animals. Thus, almost all medical schools allow students to graduate if they have done no surgery or other laboratory exercises using live animals. There is increasing discussion of these issues in veterinary schools because more and more students are becoming interested in animal rights and alternatives to animal use in veterinary education, and some schools already offer non-animal alternatives to dissection and vivisection. This information is updated on the Web site for the Association of Veterinarians for Animal Rights (www. avar.org).

The educational effectiveness of non-animal alternatives

Studies comparing the educational effectiveness of alternatives such as computer software and models show that these alternatives often are at least as good, if not better, for achieving intended educational goals. Jonathan Balcombe (1997) summarized some of these and found that for undergraduates, veterinary students, and medical students, equal knowledge or equivalent surgical skills were acquired using alternatives. The educational effectiveness of non-animal models was not less compared with animal models. For example, in a study of 2,913 first-year biology undergraduates, the examination results of 308 students who studied artificial rats were the same as those of 2,605 students who dissected real rats. When the surgical skills of 36 third-year veterinary students who trained on soft-tissue organ models were compared with the surgical skills of students who trained on dogs and cats, the performance of each group was the same. Virtual surgery has been shown to be an effective alternative. In a study of 110 medical students, students rated computer demonstrations higher for learning about cardiovascular physiology than demonstrations using dogs.[3]

What can you do?

If you are a student, you *can* request non-animal alternatives if you do not want to dissect a live earthworm, pith a frog, or

---

3. Much information about non-animal alternatives can be found at www.avar.org, www.pcrm.org (Physicians Committee for Responsible Medicine), www.hsus.org, and www.aavs.org.

work on already prepared dead specimens like cats or fetal pigs. A valid alternative is one that harms no animals. Watching others do the work is not necessarily acceptable; the alternative is one that involves no contact, either direct or indirect, with animals. As we have seen, studies show that using alternatives educates as well as or better than working on animals, and additional alternatives to animal use are continually being developed.

There also are some guidelines that might be useful if legal action becomes necessary. Gary Francione and Anna Charlton, in *Vivisection and Dissection in the Classroom* (1992), list eight steps to follow before taking legal action:

1. Know how far you are willing to go to assert your right not to engage in vivisection or dissection.
2. Raise your objection at the earliest time.
3. Whether you approach your teacher alone or with like-minded classmates, be prepared to discuss why you object to vivisection or dissection.
4. Assess the situation carefully and intelligently after you find out how receptive they are.
5. Be prepared to present one or more alternatives.
6. Document everything.
7. Seek legal help early and organize your network of support.

Finding non-animal alternatives

There are numerous ways to find out about educational alternatives. The International Network for Humane Education, (www.interniche.org) is an excellent site that's constantly updated. See also the Animalearn page at www.aavs.org/educa tion01.html. Another very useful source of alternatives can be gotten from the database known as NORINA (A Norwegian

Inventory of Audiovisuals; http://oslovet.veths.no/NORINA). Since 1991, information on over 3,500 audiovisual aids (and their suppliers) has been collected that may be used as animal alternatives or supplements in the biomedical sciences at all levels from primary school to university.

Books with information about non-animal alternatives include my *Encyclopedia of Animal Rights and Animal Welfare* (Bekoff 1998), *Animal Rights: A Beginner's Guide* (Achor 1996), and *From Guinea Pig to Computer Mouse: Alternative Methods for a Humane Education* (Jukes & Chiuia 2003).

There are centers for the development of alternatives to animals at Johns Hopkins University and the University of California at Davis, and they publish newsletters and other material concerning different alternatives. You can also call Animalearn at 1-800-SAY-AAVS (1-800-729-2287).

It is all right to question how science is taught

It's not only okay to question how science is taught—it's important to do so! Questioning how science is taught does not mean you are anti-science, anti-intellectual, or "radical." Indeed, one could argue that HAPS's position statement ("dissection and the manipulation of animal tissues and organs are essential elements in scientific investigation and introduce students to the excitement and challenge of future careers") is anti-scientific, since the data don't support it. Questioning science will make for better, more responsible science and better education.

We can decide against using animals and still have sound education. It's important to know that those who claim that non-animal alternatives do not work are simply wrong; the facts demonstrate otherwise. It is not essential to cut or kill animals to learn about life. There are *always* alternatives to cruelty.

13

Where to Go from Here?

We Are the Key to the Future

Care, share, and tread lightly

It is all too easy to talk about caring about other animals and the environment, and then walk away from the problems at hand because there will always be others who are not as busy and who will be concerned *and* act. It is too easy to pass accountability and responsibility on to others.

So, what do we need to do? It is simple—we need to ask why we continue to do the horrible things that we do to animals and ruin the environment. It is very clear that what seems to have worked in the past really has not worked at all. Some very big changes have to occur in the very near future, not when it is convenient to make them. *Time is not on our side. There is a serious sense of urgency.*

Roger Fouts—the psychologist who taught the chimpanzee Washoe to use American Sign Language—concluded in his wonderful book *Next of Kin* (1997) that "by being concerned about animals and acting on these concerns, a person is more of a healer than an activist." Of course, we are activists when we work for the well-being of animals, but perhaps more significantly, we are also helping to heal the wounds of animals who have been mistreated in the human activities I have discussed in this book.

Although not all humans feel that animals or the environment are here for us to use and abuse selfishly, human arrogance prevails in many circles. As a result, numerous animals suffer immeasurable harm because of human-centered attitudes and human domination of both animate and inanimate environments. To be sure, in order to save the precious and fragile resources on this planet, humans must place their own selfish interests aside and work with and for other life forms (including other human beings), not exploit them.

We must all live together under an umbrella of peace, working in harmony with our cohabitants on Earth, respecting them and appreciating their intrinsic value. We must make serious attempts to imagine and understand what it is like to be the animals whose lives we have been manipulating and invading— and translate this understanding into action and change. *Let's start doing this now, in whatever ways we can.*

Getting out and making a difference

There is so much you can do to help other animals and the world as a whole. This is a wonderful world, and Nature is so very generous with her gifts. Remember that there are *always* alternatives to cruelty.

Maintaining close contact with pro-animal organizations, such as the American Anti-Vivisection Society (AAVS), is a good place to start. Jane Goodall developed the Roots & Shoots program, with programs that empower young people to benefit the environment, animals, and human community in their area. The program has four global goals:

- to implement positive change through active learning about, caring for, and interacting with the environment;
- to demonstrate care and concern for all animals;
- to enhance understanding among individuals of different cultures, ethnic groups, religions, socio-economic levels, and nations through our global communications network; and
- to help young people develop self-respect, confidence in themselves, and hope for the future.

To promote learning and understanding is important because "Only when we understand can we care; only when we care shall we help; only if we help will all be saved." Every individual's efforts count, and we can each make a difference, every day, in whatever ways we choose to help. For ideas, you can also explore the Web site for the Humane Society of the United States (www.hsus.org), notably the "Animals in Research" link and the Pain & Distress campaign.

We need to talk among ourselves about the issues introduced in this book and tell family, friends, and teachers about our concerns. We can also write letters to the local media about issues concerning animals in our own areas.

In addition, we need to connect more with other animals. Even without talking, animals can be some of our best teachers about essential life lessons of love and caring. Forming bonds with animals helps us in the process of forming bonds with other humans. Especially for children and youth, contact with a companion animal is associated with improved social development, including learning to feel empathy and compassion for other children. Green Chimneys, an organization recognized as the worldwide leader in animal-assisted therapy for children with special needs, helps expose people to the benefits of developing close ties with animals.[1]

All of us—young and old—hold the key to the future. We *are* the future. Listen to your heart when it tells you that something is not right and that people or animals are being hurt.

How animals are represented in the media and entertainment

How animal images and live animals are represented in advertisements, on television, in movies, in cartoons, and in other forms of entertainment influence what people come to believe about them. Often they are given human characteristics, especially the ability to talk. They are dressed in clothes, adorned with wigs and makeup, and perform human-like actions that make people laugh. Advertisements, commercials, television programs, and movies often misleadingly portray individuals in this manner, and many people are concerned about how chimpanzees and orangutans are misrepresented as humans. They are not humans and should not be presented in this way, Jane Goodall points out: "Do you realize that the chimpanzee's smile so often seen on TV is actually a grin of fear? These trained performers suffer greatly for our amusement."

The image of the dolphin—a highly intelligent sea mammal with a playful disposition and an appealing "smile"—has also suffered distortion at the hands of humans. Consider the case of

---

1. See www.greenchimneys.org/human_animal_inter/human_animal _inter.html.

Flipper, the famous dolphin (actually there were five dolphins who played the part of Flipper) whose legend was fabricated to satisfy human desires for entertainment. Richard (Ric) O'Barry, the first trainer of Flipper, told his story in *Behind the Dolphin Smile* (1988), showing how he came to realize that keeping dolphins captive in tanks for commercial exploitation is wrong. Today, O'Barry heads the Dolphin Project, dedicated to stopping the capture and captivity of dolphins worldwide.

The mentality that humans can control and dominate animals in whatever way they want is what is behind the exploitation of the image of Flipper and the development of numerous large and very profitable businesses—including dolphin shows, each with its obligatory performing Flipper, as well as "swimming with dolphins" vacations offered to the public with no regard for how such encounters impair the lives of the animals.

A study by Elizabeth Paul (1996) at the University of Edinburgh showed that children's television programming in Great Britain promoted the notion of a hierarchy of "higher" and "lower" animals, and the belief that lower animals do not suffer as much as higher animals. Cruelty to mammals was not acceptable, but cruelty to fish and invertebrates was. Dr. Paul also found that mammals tended not to be shown as meat for human consumption, and she believes that this is because adults are uncomfortable advocating kindness to animals and then admitting that they are killed for food. They did not want their children to know that a hamburger is a cow on a bun. Nonetheless, it is important to spread this information widely.

When an animal is shown in a setting that is unrelated to its natural environment, a false message is presented. This prevents the public from gaining an accurate understanding of the animal's nature. For example, a TV commercial may include mountain lions or other wild animals to show that a sofa is soft and comfortable. When a lion is shown out of context as a soft and cuddly creature, it does nothing to promote an appreciation of the true characteristics of lions—who they are and how they live. These distortions also convey a false picture of human's place in nature and can have harmful effects in the future.

The entertainment industry has made some positive changes for the well-being of animals whom they use, but there is much more work to do. The Performing Animal Welfare Society (PAWS) has been responsible for calling attention to the abuse of animals in entertainment and doing something about it, and they, along with other groups devoted to animal welfare, have been instrumental in bringing about positive changes in the guidelines and laws that govern the use of animals in entertainment. For example, the Hollywood Office of the Humane Society of the United States is devoted to raising public awareness of animal issues by encouraging and honoring the major news and entertainment media. Through interaction with writers, producers, reporters, and compassionate celebrities—via the annual Genesis Awards and Animal Content in Entertainment—they "strive to activate the awesome power of the news and entertainment industries to influence public opinion and promote positive behavior that will ultimately lead to a more humane and animal conscious society."

Empathy: Taking the animals' point of view

Portraying animals as objects makes us think of them as commodities, things to be bought, sold, and used like property. When something goes wrong with the entertainment event, animals are too easily discarded or replaced. To counteract this false view of animals, take the animals' point of view. Imagine what their worlds are like to them. What it is like to be a bat, flying around, resting upside down, and having very sensitive hearing? Or what is it like to be a dog with a very sensitive nose and ears? Imagine what it is like to be a free-running gazelle or a wolf, coyote, or deer out in nature. Take advantage of what animals selflessly and generously offer to us. Their worlds are truly awe-inspiring. It is essential to see animals as they actually are, not as we want them to be.

It is not only ethical but enjoyable to make animals' lives better. The field biologist David W. MacDonald (1987) is proud to exclaim: "I study foxes because I am still awed by their extraordinary beauty, because they outwit me, because they keep the wind and the rain on my face ... because it is fun." Whether we are studying animals as scientists, advocating for their rights, or just enjoying nature and the company of companion animals, we can find countless ways for animals to enrich our lives that do not involved exploiting, ridiculing, or hurting them.

Now imagine what it would be like to be caged, trapped, tagged, handled, confined, restrained, isolated, shocked, mutilated, starved, deprived, dropped in hot water, or unable to escape from shock in an experiment. It is not a pretty picture.

Once again, it all comes down to speciesism, a bias that unfairly favors *Homo sapiens*. Although we are very different from other animals, is it truly believable that humans are the only species that can think, feel pain, experience anxiety, and suffer? Even if we are very different from dogs or cats, there is no reason to think that dogs, cats, and many other animals do not think in their own ways and do not feel pain and suffer in their own ways. Many people who think that *only* humans are conscious or sentient are really trying to protect their own high position on scales of nature in which humans are placed above and apart from other animals.

As Richard Ryder notes in his book *The Political Animal: The Conquest of Speciesism* (1998): "The simple truth is that we exploit the other animals and cause them suffering because we are more powerful than they are. Does that mean that if aliens land on Earth and turn out to be far more powerful than us we would let them, without argument, chase and kill us for sport, experiment on us or breed us in factory farms and turn us into tasty humanburgers? Would we accept their explanation that it is perfectly moral for them to do all these things because we are not members of their species?"

Humans cannot continue to be at war with the rest of the world. The fragility of the natural order—the delicate balance of life—requires that we all work harmoniously so as not to destroy nature's wholeness, goodness, and generosity. *Humans are a part of nature, not apart from nature.*

A compassionate ethic of caring and sharing is needed now so that the interconnectivity and spirit of the world will not be lost. In the absence of animals or even just the loss of some species, we would live in a severely impoverished, unstimulating universe. How sad this would be.

Expanding our circle of respect and understanding can help bring us all together. The community "out there" needs to become the community "in here"—in our hearts. Feelings needs to be joined with action.

Ethical enrichment

It is in the best traditions of science to ask questions about ethics. Ethics can enrich our views of other animals in their own worlds and in our different worlds, and help us to see that differences among animals are worthy of respect, admiration, and appreciation. The study of ethics can also broaden the range of possible ways in which we interact with other animals without ruining their lives. Ethical discussion can help us to see alternatives to past actions that have disrespected animals and, in the end, have not served us or other animals well. In this way, the study of ethics is enriching to both animals and humans.

In considering important ethical questions, we can discover new possibilities for how we interact with other animals. If we think that ethical considerations create unnecessary hurdles over which we must jump in order to get done what we want to get done, then we will lose rich opportunities to learn more about animals and also ourselves. *Our greatest discoveries come when our ethical relationship with other animals is respectful and not exploitive.*

The separation between "us" and "them" creates a false conflict and distances us from other life forms, eroding the many possibilities for intimate relationships among all animal life. The primatologist Barbara Smuts at the University of Michigan wrote (in Coetzee 2001): "My own life has convinced me that the limitations most of us encounter in our relations with other animals reflect not their shortcomings, as we so often assume, but our own narrow views about who they are and the kinds of relationships we can have with them."

Doing science with respect for animals: Reconciling facts with values

Studying nonhuman animals is a privilege that must not be abused. We must take this privilege seriously. Although the issues are very difficult and challenging, this does not mean they are impossible to deal with. *Certainly we cannot let animals suffer just because of our inability to come to terms with difficult issues.* Questioning the ways in which humans use animals will make for more informed decisions about animal use. By making such decisions in a responsible way, we can help ensure that in the future we will not repeat the mistakes of the past, and that we will move toward a world in which humans and other animals may be able to share peaceably the resources of a finite planet.

Thomas Dunlap, in *Saving America's Wildlife* (1988), notes that the role of science in the development and changing of ideas is highly questionable. While many people respect scientists and bestow on them special abilities to fix things when they break, scientists and science alone will not be able to deal effectively with the many difficult and puzzling problems that arise when we discuss of the nature of animal-human interactions. Personal and cultural values influence the choices we all make, and common sense also plays a large role in our decision making. In the future, science will have to incorporate values and facts and figure out how they are to be factored in to the choices we make.

Deep ethology: Respecting nature's ambassadors

I coined the term *deep ethology* (playing off the existing term *deep ecology*) to encourage people to recognize that we not only are an integral part of nature, but also have special responsibilities to nature. "Deep ethology" means respecting all animals, appreciating all animals, showing compassion for all animals, and feeling for all animals from one's heart. "Deep ethology" means resisting speciesism. A deep respect for animals does not

mean that just because animals are respected we can then do
whatever we want to them.

Our starting point should be that we will not intrude on animals' lives unless we can argue that we have a right to override
this maxim, that our actions are in the best interests of the animals irrespective of our desires. When unsure about how we
influence the lives of other animals, we should err on the side
of the animals.

Some guiding principles include:

- taking seriously the animals' points of view;
- putting respect, compassion, and admiration for other
  animals first and foremost;
- erring on the animals' side when uncertain about their
  feeling pain or suffering;
- recognizing that almost all of the methods that are
  used to study animals, even in the field, are intrusions
  on their lives—much research is exploitive;
- recognizing that speciesist assessments based on
  vague notions of an animal's cognitive or mental
  "complexity" are misguided;
- focusing on the importance of individual animals, as
  opposed to species membership;
- appreciating the variations among individual animals
  and the diversity of the lives of different individuals
  in the worlds within which they live;
- valuing common sense and empathy, even though
  traditionally these qualities have had no place in
  science; and
- using broadly based rules of loyalty and noninterven-
  tion as guiding principles.

Forming friendships and partnerships with animals

> If we want children to flourish, to become truly empowered, then let us allow them to love the earth before we ask them to save it. Perhaps this is what Thoreau had in mind when he said, "the more slowly trees grow at first, the sounder they are at the core, and I think the same is true of human beings."
> (Sobel 1996)

We and all animals with whom we share our time and space should be viewed as friends and partners in a joint venture where we enjoy an egalitarian give-and-take relationship. It is important to remember that there can be close connections among seemingly unrelated activities. Remember how logging and killing animals for bushmeat were related because hunters were able to use the roads that logging companies built to gain access to the animals they wanted to kill. Remember also how playing a guitar could be associated with killing animals and decimating fragile forests.

In our efforts to learn more about the worlds of animals, we need to study many different species. We must not be afraid of what learning about other species may bring in terms of knowledge about animal consciousness, intelligence, and their ability to feel pain and to suffer. We cannot continue to view animal suffering from afar, nor should we blind ourselves to the many ways in which we cause harm to the world around us. We have become so accustomed to the way we do things that somehow we think that we are doing just fine.

Sue Savage-Rumbaugh (1997), who is well-known for her studies of ape language with Kanzi, a male bonobo, has stressed that it is time to change course, that we need to open our eyes, our ears, our minds, our hearts. We need to *look* with a new and deeper vision, to *listen* with new and more sensitive ears. It is time to *learn* what animals are really saying to us and to one another. These three L's should inspire us to act on behalf of all animals. No person is an island, and no one can be isolated in this intimately connected universe.

What I fear the most is that if we stall in our efforts to take animal use and abuse more seriously, and if we fail to adopt extremely restrictive guidelines and laws, then even more and irreversible damage will result. Our collective regrets about what we failed to do for protecting animals' rights in the past will be beside the point. We need to enter into close and reciprocal relationships with all beings in this more-than-human world.

I hope that all animals on this planet benefit from open discussions about animal-human relationships. *When animals lose, we all lose. Every single loss diminishes us and the planet.* So when students feel that animals are being abused, they should be encouraged to call attention to these practices by talking to their teachers. Also, we should all talk to our friends and relatives and tell them what we have been discussing—it is never too late to make a change. Who knows, maybe we will learn something that we in turn can share with others.

Going to zoos or going hunting and fishing may be social events, often family activities in which parents bond with their children, but there are ways to spend family time that are not detrimental to other animals. Think about other activities in which you and your family and friends can partake, activities that are friendly to, and truly help, animals and the planet. For example, you could volunteer at the local humane society or choose a topic of interest for discussion at dinner.

We are the voices for voiceless animals: Back to the ABC'S

Remember, we are the voices for voiceless animals. Let all animals hear us, as we speak to them through our actions, showing them that we care and take their lives seriously. Nature is generous, so let us return the favor. As in most aspects of life, you receive as you give. If you give love and respect, you will receive love and respect.

So, I end as I started. Always Be Caring and Sharing—that is what the ABC'S of animal protection and compassion are all about. Making decisions about who lives and who suffers or dies is serious business. Speak out against animal abuse in zoos, circuses, rodeos, sport hunting, factory farming, various types of research, dissection and vivisection, on television, and in movies and advertising. Boycott events in which animals are abused.

Be proactive: Prevent animal abuse before it starts. Henry Spira was able to abolish the Draize Test, and public pressure greatly influenced the use of veal. Sears, Roebuck, and Company stopped sponsoring the Ringling Brother's circus in 1998 after widespread complaints about injuries and deaths of performing animals. Two people, Helen Steel and Dave Morris, were able to take on McDonald's in the longest trial in British history—dubbed the McLibel case—and show that McDonald's exploits children with their advertising, falsely advertise their food as nutritious, risk the health of their long-term regular customers, and are "culpably responsible" for cruelty to animals reared for their products.[2]

---

2. See www.mcspotlight.org and www.mcspotlight.org/case/trial/verdict/index.html.

Often, the greater our ignorance about something, the greater our resistance to change. Sometimes we are afraid of the unknown. I hope that you now know more than you did about how to protect and speak for other animals, and that you are able to make more responsible decisions after reading this book and discussing the issues with family and friends.

Remember, you hold the key to the future. You are the future. With knowledge comes growth and tolerance. Each and every one of us makes a difference. We must stroll with our animal kin, not walk away from them.

Twelve Millennial Mantras

by Marc Bekoff and Jane Goodall

In December 1999, the eve of the new millennium, we published these twelve "mantras," or principles, to serve as watchwords for the future. They are still a source of inspiration today and a compact summary of the ideals presented in this book. Our book *The Ten Trusts: What We Must Do to Care for the Animals We Love* (Goodall & Bekoff 2002) was based on these principles.

The millennium is here. Let us take stock of who we are and where we are going. Is it acceptable to weep not only for human suffering but also for the rampant misery of other animals with whom we share the planet? Can we shed tears for Sissy, the severely beaten elephant at the El Paso Zoo, the kicked and abused elephants and chimpanzee, Trudy, at the Chippenfield Circus in England? Can we also weep for the millions of animals in laboratory prisons, the billions of animals tortured and slaughtered for food and clothing? Can we sincerely mourn the destruction of the natural world, the vanishing forests, wetlands, savannas, and bodies of water? We hope these twelve mantras will make a difference for future generations:

One: Compassion and empathy for animals beget compassion and empathy for humans. Cruelty toward animals begets cruelty toward humans.

Two: All life has value and should be respected. Every animal owns her or his own life spark. Animals are not owned as property. All living creatures deserve these basic rights: the right to life, freedom from torture, and liberty to express their individual natures. Many law schools offer courses in animal law. If we agree, we would interact with animals in rather different ways. We shall need compelling reasons for denying these rights and ask forgiveness for any animal we harm.

Three: Do unto others as you would have them do unto you. Imagine what it would be like to be caged, trapped, restrained, isolated, mutilated, shocked, starved, socially deprived, hanged upside down awaiting death, or watching others slaughtered. Biological data clearly show that many animals suffer physically and psychologically and feel pain.

Four: Dominion does not mean domination. We hold dominion over animals only because of our powerful and ubiquitous intellect. Not because we are morally superior. Not because we have a "right" to exploit those who cannot defend themselves. Let us use our brain to move toward compassion and away from cruelty, to feel empathy rather than cold indifference, to feel animals' pain in our hearts.

Five: Human beings are a part of the animal kingdom, not apart from it. The separation of "us" from "them" creates a false picture and is responsible for much suffering. It is part of the in-group/out-group mentality that leads to human oppression of the weak by the strong as in ethnic, religious, political, and social conflicts. Let us open our hearts to two-way relationships with other animals, each giving and receiving. This brings pure and uncomplicated joy.

Six: To remind yourself of the importance of animals, imagine a world without them. No birdsong, no droning of nectar-searching bees, no coyotes howling, no thundering of hooves on the plains. Rachel Carson chilled our hearts with thoughts of the "silent spring." Unless we do something positive for the earth and animals, we face the prospect of silent summers, falls, and winters.

Seven: Tread lightly. Only interfere when it will be in the best interests of the animals. Imagine a world where we truly respect and admire animals, feel heartfelt empathy, compassion, and understanding. Imagine how we would be freed of guilt, conscious or unconscious in such a world.

Eight: Make ethical choices in what we buy, do, and watch. In a consumer-driven society our individual choices, used collectively for the good of animals and nature, can change the world faster than laws.

Nine: Have the courage of conviction. Never say never. Act now. Be proactive; prevent animal abuse before it starts. Dare to speak out to save the world's precious and fragile resources. Live as much as possible in harmony with nature, respecting the intrinsic value of all life and the wondrous composition of earth, water, and air.

Ten: Every individual matters and has a role to play. Our actions make a difference. Public pressure has been responsible for much social change, including more humane treatment of animals. "Whistle blowers" have courageously revealed intolerable conditions in laboratories, circuses, slaughterhouses, and so on, often at the expense of their jobs. Henry Spira organized peaceful demonstrations that led to questioning the Draize Test, in which rabbits are harmed to learn about the effects of eye shadow. His efforts also led to the formation of centers devoted to the development of non-animal alternatives, sponsored by the cosmetic companies themselves. Public pressure greatly reduced veal consumption and led to Sears, Roebuck, and Company ending their sponsorship of Ringling Brothers Barnum & Bailey Circus. Helen Steel and Dave Morris took on McDonald's in the longest trial in British history (the "McLibel" case) and showed that McDonald's exploits children with their advertising and are "culpably responsible" for cruelty to animals.

Eleven: Be a passionate visionary, a courageous crusader. Combat cruelty and catalyze compassion. Do not fear to express love. Do not fear to be too generous or too kind. Above all, understand that there are many reasons to remain optimistic even when things seem grim. Let us harness the indomitable human spirit. Together we can make this a better world for all living organisms. We must, for our children, and theirs. We must stroll with our kin, not walk away from them.

A millennial mantra: When animals lose, we all lose. Every single loss diminishes us as well as the magnificent world in which we live together.

References and Resources

Here is a list of general resource material covering many of the issues discussed in this book. This list includes books and articles that are frequently cited in the book, as well as journals that publish essays concerned with animal rights, environmental ethics, and animal behavior, cognition, and emotions.

Numerous references and organizations that deal with animal protection can be found in the following sources:

Achor, A. B. 1992. *Animal Rights: A Beginners Guide.* Yellow Springs, OH: Writeware.

Animals' Agenda, www.animalsagenda.org/DirOrgLinks.asp?menu =DirOrgLinks.

Bekoff, M., ed. 1998. *Encyclopedia of Animal Rights and Animal Welfare.* Westport, CT: Greenwood Publishing Group.

Organizations and Web Sites

Alliance for Bio-integrity, www.biointegrity.org
American Anti-Vivisection Society (AAVS), www.aavs.org
Animalearn, www.animalearn.org; www.aavs.org/education01.html
Animal Protection Institute, www.api4animals.org
Animal Rights International, www.ari-online.org
Association of Veterinarians for Animal Rights, www. avar.org
Association of Zoos and Aquariums, www.aza.org

The Bushmeat Project, http://bushmeat.net
Chimpanzees in research: http://first100chimps.wesleyan.edu
Cruelty-free information:
    www.allforanimals.com/cruelfree1.htm
    www.buav.org/gocrueltyfree/index.html
    www.caringconsumer.com
The Dolphin Project, www.dolphinproject.org
Envirolink: The Online Environmental Community, www.enviroweb.org
Ethologists for the Ethical Treatment of Animals, www.ethological ethics.org
First Strike. *See* Humane Society of the United States.
Genetic engineering links: www.safe-food.org
The Great Ape Project, www.greatapeproject.org
Green Chimneys Children's Services: Restoring Possibilities for Children through Nurture and Nature, www.greenchimneys.org
Humane Farming Association, www.hfa.org
Humane Society of the United States (HSUS), www.hsus.org
In Defense of Animals, www.idausa.org
Institute for Humane Education, http://humaneeducation.org
International Network for Humane Education, www.interniche.org
The Jane Goodall Institute, www.janegoodall.org
Organic Consumers Association, www.organicconsumers.org
People for the Ethical Treatment of Animals (PETA), www.peta.org
The Performing Animal Welfare Society (PAWS), www.pawsweb.org
Roots & Shoots: A Program of the Jane Goodall Institute, www.rootsandshoots.org

Books, Reports, and Pamphlets

Abram, D. 1996. *The spell of the sensuous: Perception and language in a more-than-human world.* New York: Pantheon Books.
Achor, A. B. 1996. *Animal rights: A beginner's guide.* Yellow Springs, OH: WriteWare.
Adams, C. J. 1994. *Neither man nor beast: Feminism and the defense of animals.* New York: Continuum.
Allen, C. 1998. Assessing animal cognition: Ethological and philosophical perspectives. *Journal of Animal Science* 76: 42–47.
Allen, C., and M. Bekoff. 1997. *Species of mind: The philosophy and biology of cognitive ethology.* Cambridge: MIT Press.

Animal Welfare Institute. 1990. *Animals and their legal rights.* Washington, D.C.

Baird, R. M., and S. E. Rosenbaum, eds. 1991. *Animal experimentation: The moral issues.* Buffalo, NY: Prometheus Books.

Balcombe, J. 1997. Student/teacher conflict regarding animal dissection. *The American Biology Teacher* 59: 22–25.

Balcombe, J. 1999. *The use of animals in higher education: Problems, alternatives, and recommendations.* Washington, D.C.: HSUS.

———. 2007. *Pleasurable kingdom: Animals and the nature of feeling good.* New York: Macmillan.

Balls, M., et al. 1995. *The Three Rs: The way forward: The report and recommendations of ECVAM (European Centre for the Validation of Alternative Methods) workshop. ATLA (Alternatives to Laboratory Animals)* 23: 838–866.

Bateson, P. P. G. 1997. The behavioural and physiological effects of culling red deer. Report to the Council of the National Trust. London.

Bayne, K. A. L., and M. D. Kreger, eds. 1995. *Wildlife mammals as research models: In the laboratory and field.* Greenbelt, MD: Scientists Center for Animal Welfare.

Bekoff, M. 1994. Cognitive ethology and the treatment of non-human animals: How matters of mind inform matters of welfare. *Animal Welfare* 3: 75–96.

———. 1995. Marking, trapping, and manipulating animals: Some methodological and ethical considerations. In Bayne & Kreger 1995, pp. 31–47.

———. 1996. Are dissection and tissue and organ manipulation really essential? *Strategies* (Spring) pp. 4–5.

———. 1998a. Deep ethology. *AV Magazine* (A publication of the American Anti-Vivisection Society) 106, no. 1 (Winter): 10–18.

———. 1998b. Deep ethology, animal rights, and the Great Ape/Animal Project: Resisting speciesism and expanding the community of equals. *Journal of Agricultural and Environmental Ethics* 10: 269–296.

———. 1998c. Resisting speciesism and expanding the community of equals. *BioScience* 48: 638–641.

———. 2000. Human-carnivore interactions: Adopting proactive strategies for complex problems. In J. L. Gittleman, S. M. Funk,

D. W. Macdonald, and R. K. Wayne (eds.), *Carnivore conservation*. London: Cambridge University Press.

———. 2002. *Minding animals: Awareness, emotions, and heart.* New York: Oxford University Press.

———. 2007. *The emotional lives of animals: A leading scientist explores animal joy, sorrow, and empathy—and why they matter.* Novato, CA: New World Library.

Bekoff, M., ed. 1998. *Encyclopedia of animal rights and animal welfare.* Westport, CT: Greenwood Publishing Group.

———, ed. 2000. *The smile of a dolphin: Remarkable accounts of animal emotions.* New York: Random House/Discovery Books.

———, ed. 2007. *Encyclopedia of human-animal relationships: A global exploration of our connections with animals.* Westport, CT: Greenwood Publishing Group.

Bekoff, M., and D. Jamieson. 1996. Ethics and the study of carnivores. In J. L. Gittleman (ed.), *Carnivore behavior, ecology, and evolution.* Ithaca, NY: Cornell University Press, pp. 16–45.

Berry, T. 1999. *The great work: Our way into the future.* New York: Bell Tower.

Biederman, P. W. 2004. Soft under her thick skin? *Los Angeles Times,* November 16.

Bostock, S. St.C. 1993. *Zoos and animal rights.* London: Routledge.

Bowen-Jones, E., and S. Pendry. 1999. The threat to primates and other mammals from the bushmeat trade in Africa, and how this threat could be diminished. *Oryx* 33: 233–246.

Callicott, J. B. 1980. Animal liberation: A triangular affair. In J. B. Callicott, *In defense of the land ethic: Essays in environmental philosophy.* Albany: State University of New York Press, 1989, pp. 15–38.

Campbell, T. Colin. 2005. *The China study: The most comprehensive study of nutrition ever conducted and the startling implications for diet, weight loss and long-term health.* Dallas: Benbella Books.

Campbell, T. C., and J. Chen. 1994. Diet and chronic degenerative diseases: Perspectives from China. *American Journal of Clinical Nutrition* 59: 1153–61.

Carbone, L. 2004. *What animals want: Expertise and advocacy in laboratory animal welfare policy.* New York: Oxford University Press.

Carson, R. 1962. *Silent Spring.* Boston: Houghton-Mifflin.

Cavalieri, P., and P. Singer, eds. 1993. *The Great Ape Project: Equality beyond humanity.* London: Fourth Estate.

Coetzee, J. M. 2001. *The lives of animals.* Princeton, NJ: Princeton University Press.

Collard, S. B., III. 2000. *Acting for nature: What young people around the world have done to protect the environment.* Berkeley: Heyday Books.

Crick, F. 1994. *The astonishing hypothesis: The scientific search for soul.* New York: Scribners.

Croke, V. 1997. *The modern ark: The story of zoos: Past, present, and future.* New York: Scribners.

Darwin, C. 2004. *The descent of man* (1871). New York: Penguin Classics.

Dauncey, G. 2007. *Building an ark: 101 solutions to animal suffering.* Gabriola Island, BC: New Society Publishers.

Davis, H., and D. Balfour, eds. 1992. *The inevitable bond: Examining scientist-animal interactions.* New York: Cambridge University Press.

Davis, K. 1996. *Poisoned chickens, poisoned eggs: An inside look at the modern poultry industry.* Summertown, TN: Book Publishing Company.

Davis, S. G. 1997. *Spectacular nature: Corporate culture and the Sea World experience.* Berkeley: University of California Press.

Dawkins, M. S. 1980. *Animal suffering: The science of animal welfare.* New York: Chapman and Hall.

———. 1993. *Through our eyes only?* San Francisco: W. H. Freeman.

DeGrazia, D. 1996. *Taking animals seriously: Mental life and moral status.* New York: Cambridge University Press.

———. 1999. Animal ethics around the turn of the twenty-first century. *Journal of Agricultural and Environmental Ethics* 11: 111–129.

Dickinson, P. 1988. *Eva.* New York: Dell.

Dol, M.; S. Kasamoentalib; S. Lijmbach; E. Rivas; and R. van den Bos, eds. *Animal consciousness and animal ethics.* Assen, the Netherlands: Van Gorcum.

Drayer, M. E., ed. 1997. *The animal dealers: Evidence of abuse of animals in the commercial trade 1952–1997.* Washington, D.C.: Animal Welfare Institute.

Duda, M. D.; S. J. Bissell; and K. C. Young. 1996. Factors related to hunting and fishing participation in the United States. *Transactions of the 61st American Wildlife and Natural Resources Conference,* pp. 324–337.

Dunlap, T. R. 1988. *Saving America's wildlife: Ecology and the American mind.* Princeton, NJ: Princeton University Press.

Eisnitz, G. A. 1997. *Slaughterhouse: The shocking story of greed, neglect, and inhumane treatment inside the U. S. meat industry.* Buffalo, NY: Prometheus Books.

Fano, A. 1997. *Lethal laws: Animal testing, human health and environmental policy.* London: Zed Books.

Finsen, L., and A. Finsen, 1994. *The animal rights movement in American: From compassion to respect.* New York: Twayne Publishers.

Fouts, R., with S. Mills. 1997. *Next of kin: What chimpanzees have taught me about who we are.* New York: William Morrow and Company.

Fox, M. A. 1998. Vegetarianism. In Bekoff 1998.

———. 1999. *Deep vegetarianism.* Philadelphia: Temple University Press.

Fox, M. W. 1980. *Returning to Eden: Animal rights and human responsibility.* New York: Viking Press.

———. 1990. *Inhumane society: The American way of exploiting animals.* New York: St. Martin's Press.

———. 1992. *Superpigs and wondercorn.* New York: Lyons and Burford.

———. 1997. *Eating with conscience: The bioethics of food.* Troutdale, OR: NewSage Press.

———. 1999. *Beyond evolution: The genetically altered future of plants, animals, the earth . . . and humans.* New York: Lyons Press.

Francione, G. L. 1995. *Animals, property, and the law.* Philadelphia: Temple University Press.

———. 1996. *Rain without thunder: The ideology of the animal rights movement.* Philadelphia: Temple University Press.

———. 1999. *Introduction to animal rights: Your child or the dog?* Philadelphia: Temple University Press.

Francione, G. L., and A. E. Charlton. 1992. *Vivisection and dissection in the classroom: A guide to conscientious objection.* Jenkintown, PA: American Anti-Vivisection Society.

Fraser, L. 1990. *The animal rights handbook: Everyday ways to save animal lives.* Los Angeles: Living Planet Press.

Gentle, M. J. 1992. Pain in birds. *Animal Welfare* 1: 237–247.

Gibbons, E. F.; E. J. Wyers; E. Waters; and E. W. Menzel, eds. 1994. *Naturalistic environments in captivity for animal behavior research.* Albany: State University of New York Press.

Gibbons, E. F., Jr.; B. S. Durrant; and J. Demarest, eds. 1995. *Conservation of endangered species in captivity.* Albany: State University of New York Press.

Godlovitch, S. and R., and J. Harris, eds. 1972. *Animals, men and morals.* New York: Taplinger.

Gold, M. 1995. *Animal rights: Extending the circle of compassion.* Oxford: Jon Carpenter.

Goodall, J. 1990. *Through a window: My thirty years with the chimpanzees of Gombe.* Boston: Houghton Mifflin Company.

———. 1994. Digging up the roots. *Orion* 13: 20–21.

Goodall, J., and M. Bekoff. 2002. *The ten trusts: What we must do to care for the animals we love.* San Francisco: HarperSanFrancisco.

Goodall, J., with P. Berman. 1999. *Reason for hope: A spiritual journey.* New York: Warner Books.

Goodman, B. 1991. Keeping anglers happy has a price: Ecological and genetic effects of stocking fish. *BioScience* 41: 294–299.

Goude, A., ed. 1994. *The human impact on the natural environment.* Cambridge: MIT Press.

Greek, R., and J. Greek. 2000. *Sacred cows and golden geese: The human costs of experiments on animals.* New York: Continuum.

Green, A. 1999. *Animal underworld: Inside America's market for rare and exotic species.* New York: PublicAffairs.

Guillermo, K. S. 1993. *Monkey business: The disturbing case that launched the animal rights movement.* Washington, D.C.: National Press Books.

Harlow, H. F. 1959. Love in infant monkeys. *Scientific American* 200, no. 6 (June): 68–74.

Hart, L., ed. 1998. *Responsible conduct of research in animal behavior.* New York: Oxford University Press.

Hoage, R. J., ed. 1989. *Perceptions of animals in American culture.* Washington, D.C.: Smithsonian Institution Press.

Jamieson, D. 1985. Against zoos. In Peter Singer (ed.), *In defense of animals.* New York: Basil Blackwell, pp. 108–117; www.animal-rights-library.com/texts-m/jamieson01.htm.

Johnson, A. 1992. *Factory farming.* New York: Basil Blackwell.

Johnson, L. E. 1991. *A morally deep world: An essay on moral significance and environmental ethics.* New York: Cambridge University Press.

Jukes, N., and M. Chiuia. 2003. *From guinea pig to computer mouse: Alternative methods for a humane education.* 2nd ed. Leicester, England: InterNICHE.

Kahn, P. H., Jr. 1999. *The human relationship with nature: Development and culture.* Cambridge: MIT Press.

Kellert, S. R., and E. O. Wilson, eds. 1993. *The biophilia hypothesis.* Washington, D.C.: Island Press.

Kew, B. 1991. *The pocketbook of animal facts and figures.* London: Green Print.

Kirkwood, J. 1992. Wild animal welfare. In R. D. Ryder and P. Singer (eds.), *Animal welfare and the environment.* London: Duckworth, pp. 139–154.

Kistler, J., ed. 2000. *Animal rights: Subject guide, bibliography, and internet companion.* Westport, CT: Greenwood Publishing Group.

Kleiman, D. G.; M. E. Allen; K. V. Thompson; and S. Lumpkin, eds. 1996. *Wild mammals in captivity: Principles and techniques.* Chicago: University of Chicago Press.

Knight, R. L., and K. J. Gutzwiller, eds. 1995. *Wildlife and recreationists: Coexistence through management and research.* Washington, D.C.: Island Press.

Krause, M. 1996. Biological continuity and great ape rights. *Animal Law* 2: 171–178.

LaFollette, H., and N. Shanks. 1996. *Brute science: The dilemmas of animal experimentation.* New York: Routledge.

Lauck, J. E. 2002. *The voice of the infinite in the small: Re-visioning the insect-human connection.* Boston: Shambhala Publications.

Linzey, A. 1976. *Animal rights.* London: SCM Press.

Lockwood, R., and F. R. Ascione, eds. 1998. *Cruelty to animals and interpersonal violence: Readings in research and application.* West Lafayette, IN: Purdue University Press.

Lorenz, K. 1992. *Here I am—where are you? The behavior of the greylag goose.* New York: HarperCollins.

Lyman, H. F. 1998. *Mad cowboy: Plain truth from the cattle rancher who won't eat meat.* New York: Scribner.

MacDonald, D. W. 1987. *Running with the fox.* New York: Facts on File.

Mack, A., ed. 1999. *Humans and other animals.* Columbus: Ohio State University Press.

Magel, C. R. 1989. *Keyguide to information sources in animal rights.* Jefferson, NC: McFarland.

Manes, C. 1997. *Other creations: Rediscovering the spirituality of animals.* New York: Doubleday.

Manning, A., and J. Serpell, eds. 1994. *Animals and human society: Changing perspectives.* New York: Routledge.

Martin, A. N. 1997. *Foods pets die for: Shocking facts about pet food.* Troutdale, OR: NewSage Press.

Mason, J. 1993. *An unnatural order: Uncovering the roots of our domination of nature and each other.* New York: Simon & Schuster.

Mason, J., and P. Singer. 1980. *Animal factories.* New York: Crown.

Masson, J. M., and S. McCarthy. 1995. *When elephants weep: The emotional lives of animals.* New York: Delacourte Press.

Medical Research Modernization Committee. 1998. A critical look at animal experimentation. P.O. Box 2751, New York, NY 10163-2751.

Meyers, G. 1998. *Children and animals: Social development and our connections to other species.* Boulder: Westview Press.

Midgley, M. 1983. *Animals and why they matter.* Athens: University of Georgia Press.

Mighetto, L. 1991. *Wild animals and American environmental ethics.* Tucson: University of Arizona Press.

Newkirk, I. 1998. *Kids can save the animals! 101 easy things to do.* New York: Warner Books.

———. 2006. *Fifty awesome ways kids can help animals: Fun and easy ways to be a kind kid.* New York: Warner Books.

Nichols, M., and J. Goodall. 1999. *Brutal kinship.* New York: Aperture.

O'Barry, R., with K. Coulbourn. 1988. *Behind the dolphin smile.* Chapel Hill, NC: Algonquin Books.

Orion Society. 1995. *Bringing the world alive: A bibliography of nature stories for children.* Great Barrington, MA: Orion Society.

Orlans, F. B. 1993. *In the name of science: Issues in responsible animal experimentation.* New York: Oxford University Press.

Orlans, F. B.; T. L. Beauchamp; R. Dresser; D. B. Morton; and J. P. Gluck, eds. 1998. *The human use of animals: Case studies in ethical choice.* New York: Oxford University Press.

Paul, E. S. 1996. The representation of animals on children's television. *Anthrozoös* 9: 169–181.

Peterson, D. 2003. *Eating apes.* Berkeley: University of California Press.

Peterson, D., and J. Goodall. 1993. *Visions of Caliban: On chimpanzees and people.* Boston: Houghton Mifflin Company.

Pluhar, E. B. 1995. *Beyond prejudice: The moral significance of human and non-human animals.* Durham, NC: Duke University Press.

Poole, J. 1998. An exploration of a commonality between ourselves and elephants. *Etica & Animali* 9: 85–110.

Puppe, B.; P.-Ch. Schön; A. Tuchscherer; and G. Manteuffel. 2005. Castration-induced vocalisation in domestic piglets, *Sus scrofa*: Complex and specific alterations of the vocal quality. *Applied Animal Behavioral Science* 95: 67–78.

Quinn, D. *Ishmael.* New York: Bantam.

Rachels, J. 1990. *Created from animals: The moral implications of Darwinism.* New York: Oxford University Press.

Regan, T. 1983. *The case for animal rights.* Berkeley: University of California Press.

Regan, T., and P. Singer, eds. 1989. *Animal rights and human obligations.* 2nd ed. Englewood Cliffs, NJ: Prentice-Hall.

Regenstein, L. G. 1991. *Replenish the earth: A history of organized religion's treatment of animals and nature—including the Bible's message of conservation and kindness toward animals.* New York: Crossroad.

Rivera, M. A. 2004. *Canines in the classroom: Raising humane children through interactions with animals.* New York: Lantern Books.

Rollin, B. E. 1989. *The unheeded cry: Animal consciousness, animal pain and science.* New York: Oxford University Press. Reissued 1998 by Iowa State University Press.

———. 1992. *Animal rights and human morality* (1981). Rev. ed. Buffalo, NY: Prometheus Books.

———. 1995. *The Frankenstein syndrome: Ethical and social issues in the genetic engineering of animals.* New York: Cambridge University Press.

Rolston, H., III. 1989. *Environmental ethics: Duties to and values in the natural world.* Philadelphia: Temple University Press.

Rowan, A. 1984. *Of mice, models, and men: A critical evaluation of animal research.* Albany: State University of New York Press.

Rowan, A., ed. 1988. *Animals and people sharing the world.* Hanover, NH: University Press of New England.

Rowan, A. N.; F. M. Loew; and J. C. Weer. 1995. *The animal research controversy: Protest, process and public policy—an analysis of strategic issues.* Boston: Tufts University School of Veterinary Medicine.

Rowe, M., ed. 1999. *The way of compassion: Survival strategies for a world in crisis.* New York: Stealth Technologies.

Russell, W. M. S., and R. L. Burch. 1992. *The principles of humane experimental technique* (1959). Wheathampstead, England: Universities Federation for Animal Welfare.

Ryder, R. D. 1989. *Animal revolution: Changing attitudes towards speciesism.* London: Blackwell.

———. 1998. *The political animal: The conquest of speciesism.* Jefferson, NC, & London: McFarland & Company.

Sapontzis, S. 1995. We should not allow dissection of animals. *Journal of Agricultural and Environmental Ethics* 8: 181–189.

Savage-Rumbaugh. E. S. 1997. Why are we afraid of apes with language? In A. B. Scheibel and J. W. Schopf (eds.), *Origin and evolution of intelligence.* Sudbury, MA: Jones and Bartlett, pp. 43–69.

Schaller, G. B. 1993. *The last panda.* Chicago: University of Chicago Press.

Shapiro, K. 1998. *Animal models of human psychology: Critique of science, ethics and policy.* Seattle: Hogrefe & Huber Publishers.

Shepherdson, D. J.; J. D. Mellen; and M. Hutchins, eds. 1998. *Second nature: Environmental enrichment for captive animals.* Washington, D.C.: Smithsonian Institution Press.

Singer, P. 1990. *Animal liberation.* 2nd ed. New York: New York Review of Books.

———. 1998. *Ethics into action: Henry Spira and the animal rights movement.* Lanham, MD: Rowman & Littlefield.

Singer, P., ed. 1986. *In defense of animals.* New York: Harper and Row.

Sobel, D. 1996. *Beyond ecophobia: Reclaiming the heart in nature education.* Great Barrington, MA: Orion Society.

Sowing seeds: A humane education workbook. 1995. Animalearn and LivingEarth Learning Project. Jenkintown, PA: American Anti-Vivisection Society.

Spira, H. 1986. Fighting to win. In Singer 1986, pp. 194–208.

Stephens, M. L. 1986. *Maternal deprivation experiments in psychology: A critique of animal models.* Jenkintown, PA: American Anti-Vivisection Society.

Tannenbaum, J. 1995. *Veterinary Ethics.* 2nd ed. St. Louis, MO: Mosby.

Taylor, P. W. 1986. *Respect for nature: A theory of environmental ethics.* Princeton, NJ: Princeton University Press.

Thanki, D. 1998. Virtual surgery in veterinary medicine. *Animal Welfare Information Center Newsletter* 9 (nos. 1–2): 11.

Tobias, M. 1998. *Nature's keepers: On the front lines of the fight to save wildlife in America.* New York: John Wiley.

———. 1999. *Voices from the underground: For the love of animals.* Pasadena, CA: Hope Publishing House.

Tobias M., and J. Morrison. 2006. *Donkey: The mystique of Equus asinus.* Tulsa, OK: Council Oak Books.

Tobias, M., and K. Solisti, eds. 1998. *Kinship with the animals.* Portland, OR: Beyond Words Publishers.

Weil, Z. 2003. *Above all, be kind: Raising a humane child in challenging times.* Gabriola Island, BC: New Society Publishers.

———. 2004. *The Power and Promise of Humane Education.* Gabriola Island, BC: New Society Publishers.

Wemelsfeder F., and M. Farish. 2004. Qualitative categories for the interpretation of sheep welfare: A review. *Animal Welfare* 13: 261–268.

Wemelsfelder, F.; E. A. Hunter; M. T. Mendl; and A. B. Lawrence. 2000. The spontaneous qualitative assessment of behavioural expressions in pigs: First explorations of a novel methodology for integrative animal welfare measurement. *Applied Animal Behaviour Science* 67: 193–215.

Wemelsfelder, F., and A. B. Lawrence. 2001. Qualitative assessment of animal behaviour as an on-farm welfare-monitoring tool. *Acta Agriculturae Scandinavica* 30: 21–25 (supplement).

Wilcove, D. S.; D. Rothstein; J. Dubow; A. Phillips; and E. Losos. 1998. Quantifying threats to imperiled species in the United States. *BioScience* 48: 607–615.

Wilkie, D. S. 1999. Bushmeat hunting in the Congo Basin: An assessment of impacts and options for mitigation. *Biodiversity and Conservation* 8: 927–955.

Wise, S. M. 2000. *Rattling the cage: Toward legal rights for animals.* Cambridge, MA: Perseus Books.

Woodroffe, R.; J. Ginsberg; and D. Macdonald. 1997. *The African wild dog.* Gland, Switzerland: International Union for Conservation of Nature and Natural Resources.

Wynne-Tyson, J., ed. 1988. *The extended circle: A commonplace book of animal rights.* New York: Paragon House.

Zimmerman, M. E.; J. B. Callicott; G. Sessions; K. J. Warren; and J. Clark, eds. 1993. *Environmental philosophy: From animal rights to radical ecology.* New York: Prentice-Hall.

Zurlo, J.; D. Rudacille; and A. M. Goldberg. 1994. *Animals and alternatives testing: History, science, and ethics.* New York: Mary Ann Liebert.

Glossary

animal models. A model is an analogy or example that can be used to study something similar to it. Thus, scientists use experiments with animals as models of human disease by designing controlled experiments in which animals are made ill and then the course of the disease and its treatment are studied. The intention is to draw conclusions that can be applied to humans with the same disease. Animals are used instead of humans because it would not be ethical to make human beings sick or even die for the sake of a study. The question raised in this book is whether it is ethical to use animals in this way, subjecting them to cruel procedures that cause pain, suffering, and death. Another objection to animal models is that statistics show they often do not apply accurately to humans and offer little success in solving human problems.

animal rights. The position that animals have certain moral and legal rights, including the right not to be harmed. Rightists believe that it is wrong to cause animals any pain and suffering, and that animals should not be eaten, used for clothing, held captive in zoos, subjected to painful experiments, or used in most or any research.

animal welfare. A position concerned with the well-being of animals without conceding that animals have rights. Welfarists believe it is all right to use animals for human benefit as long as humane safeguards are used to ensure protection from unnecessary or undue suffering. Unlike animal rightists, they accept the humane use of animals in experiments and the slaughtering of animals as food for humans.

anthropomorphism. Using human characteristics to describe or explain the feelings or behavior of a nonhuman. Traditionally, anthropomorphic language has been discouraged in the sciences because it is considered subjective, overly personal, and misleading. For example, many people consider it anthropomorphic to attribute human emotions to an animal, claiming, say, that two dogs are "in love" or that a singing bird is joyous. However, because there are similarities, or *evolutionary continuity,* between animals and humans, anthropomorphism often makes sense. It allows animals' behavior and emotions to be accessible to us and helps us to understand their points of view. *See also* biocentric anthropomorphism.

anti-vivisection. Opposition to experimentation on animals and other forms of cruelty to animals. Vivisection is the cruel practice of cutting or operating on a live animal.

biocentric anthropomorphism. Anthropomorphism that takes into account the perceptual world and neural architecture (that is correlated with cognitive and emotional capacities) of members of a given species, so that the animal's point of view is not ignored.

biodiversity. The number of different animal and plant species that inhabit our planet or a particular ecosystem. As species become extinct, there is much concern about the loss of biodiversity, which is often traced to human actions that caused as disruption of animal populations in the first place. Ethical controversies arise over how much humans should intervene in nature in an attempt to maintain or restore the diversity of life forms. For example, should we capture individual animals of endangered species, bred them in captivity, and then release them back into their former habitats?

bushmeat. The meat of wild animals killed for food for humans and sold in an illegal profit-making commercial trade, especially in Africa. Murdering animals for their meat often means that infants are orphaned when their mothers are killed. The practice is not only cruel but also threatens the survival of several species, including monkeys, great apes (bonobos, chimpanzees, and gorillas), crocodiles, elephants, and guinea fowl.

cloning. Reproductive cloning is a technology for creating an animal that has the same genetic identity as an already existing animal. Scientists perform cloning by transferring genetic material (DNA) from a donor cell to an egg whose DNA has been removed. Once the resulting embryo develops to a certain stage, it can be implanted in the body of a female animal who will carry it and give birth to the cloned animal. Ethical concerns have made cloning a controversial practice. *See also* genetic engineering.

cognition. The various aspects of the mind at work, including consciousness, self-awareness, intelligence, thought, judgment, and decision making.

cognitive ethology. The comparative, evolutionary, and ecological study of animal minds. This science focuses on how animals think and what they feel, including their emotions, beliefs, reasoning, information processing, consciousness, and self-awareness. Cognitive ethologists are interested in tracing the mental continuity among different species; learning how and why intellectual skills and emotions evolve; and understanding what it is like to be a particular animal. *See also* deep ethology.

companion animal. An animal kept by a person for companionship rather than purely utilitarian reasons. Many people use the term *companion animal* because it implies a mutual, respectful relationship with an animal, as opposed to pet, which suggests that the animal is merely there to be petted.

compassion. An emotion associated with sensitivity to the suffering of others, combined with a desire to relieve their pain. Choosing compassion over cruelty toward animals is an important principle, along with offering them empathy and respect. Animals themselves also demonstrate compassion, as when a group of elephants patiently wait for a lame elephant to catch up with them, or when a mouse writhes in empathy with another mouse in pain. *See also* empathy.

costs and benefits. An approach to evaluating a given action by weighing its advantages against its disadvantages. The utilitarian approach to animal welfare seeks to maximize benefits to humans while reducing costs to animals.

cruelty-free. A term referring to products (such as cosmetics) that have not been tested on animals and do not contain ingredients derived from wildlife or with processes that harm animals.

These products are usually labeled "cruelty-free" or "not tested on animals" and may sport a bunny logo or similar symbol.

deep ethology. A term coined by Marc Bekoff for a branch of the science of ethology, the study of animal behavior. Deep ethology represents a deepening of conventional ethology because it introduces the element of human responsibility for animals: our recognition that animals have emotions, feelings of pain and suffering, and the right to our respect, empathy, and compassion. In deep ethology, the data collected by scientists are used for the betterment of animals, because animals matter.

dissection. Cutting or separating the parts of a dead animal in order to study the tissue. The practice of dissection in science classes and other educational settings is controversial. In this book we have argued in favor of non-animal alternatives to this cruel practice.

Draize Test. A test used by companies to determine whether cosmetic and household products will cause eye irritation. Drops of the substance being tested are placed in the eyes of rabbits. After suffering injuries such as ulcers and blindness, the animals are killed. The test was named for John Draize, an FDA scientist, who standardized the scoring system of a preexisting test in 1944. It has been protested as being cruel and also inconclusive, since the rabbit's eye is different from the human eye.

empathy. An emotional capacity that enables us to understand another individual's feelings from his or her own point of view. If you know how another person feels, or can imagine what it might be like to experience the world of a bat, a dog, or an eagle, then you are feeling empathy. (Empathy is similar to sympathy, although the latter suggests feeling sorry for another individual who is suffering.) Empathy for animals is an important quality for us to bring to decision making about humans' relationships with the animal world. Studies show that many nonhuman animals also display empathy for one another. *See also* compassion.

endangered. The term *endangered* is applied to plants or animals that are in danger of becoming extinct (the last existing member of that species dies). The United States and other countries have laws protecting endangered animals. Which animals are listed as endangered is determined by evaluating how many individuals remain and whether or not they are able to reproduce. The

International Union for the Conservation of Nature and Natural Resources (IUCN) Red List, begun in 1963, is the most comprehensive inventory of the status of a given species.

enrichment. Methods of providing a stimulating environment that will reduce boredom for captive animals and on occasion make their living situation closer to their natural habitat. Examples include hiding the animals' food to give them the challenge of finding it, and providing exercise wheels for caged animals.

environmental philosophy. A branch of philosophy concerned with ethical relationships between humans and the natural environment.

ethics. A branch of philosophy concerned with issues of rightness or fairness and how we should behave toward others. An "ethic" (in the singular) means a set of principles or values that guide an activity; for example, the ethical values that govern how scientific research is conducted with animals would determine a *research ethic.*

ethology. The scientific study of animal behavior that takes into account the natural (or evolved) behavior of individuals of a given species. Careful attention is given to questions centering on evolution (why and how a behavior pattern has evolved), adaptation (how the performance of a specific behavior allows an individual to adapt to his or her environment and how that influences reproductive success), causation (what causes a specific behavior to be performed), and development (how a behavior unfolds and changes during an individual's lifetime). *See also* cognitive ethology; deep ethology.

evolutionary continuity. The Darwinian view that evolution takes place along a continuum, so that certain characteristics are continuous from one species to the next. The idea that differences among species are differences in degree rather than in kind argues strongly for the presence of emotions, empathy, and moral behavior in animals.

factory farming. The commercial mass-production of animal foods such as poultry, eggs, and dairy products, as well as crops. Opponents of factory farming point to the horrifically inhumane conditions in which animals are raised for food, as well as various practices (such as using pesticides and hormones) that are unsafe for humans who eat the food products and harmful to the environment.

genetic engineering. A scientific technology for manipulating the genes of a plant or animal in order to create desired characteristics in the offspring. Genetic engineering is controversial for many different reasons. Some people think it is morally wrong to interfere with natural reproductive processes. Others feel that genetic engineering could lead to unforeseen health problems for humans, as when plants or animals food are genetically modified in an attempt to improve food products. Much laboratory research involves genetically altering animals' cells, which may be considered cruel treatment of those individuals. *Cloning* is a form of genetic engineering.

great apes. The great apes are primates who are members of the biological family Hominidae, which includes humans, chimpanzees, bonobos, gorillas, and orangutans. Movements such as the Great Ape Project have been launched to improve the lives of these magnificent animals and to eliminate their use in scientific research, in exploitative entertainment, and as food. *See also* bushmeat.

instrument effect. In a test or experiment, the effect of equipment, instruments, and techniques, causing the results to be misleading. For example, when penguins dive under water, their behavior is changed when they have to wear a device on their back that shows how fast they have dived and how deep they have gone.

invertebrates. Animals without a backbone (vertebrae). Invertebrates include worms, insects, snails, and various sea creatures such as octopuses, starfish, and jellyfish. Some people believe that invertebrates do not experience pain the way vertebrates do. However, some invertebrates possess nerve cells that are associated with the feeling of pain. This book argues that we should assume that all animals can experience pain and treat them accordingly. *See also* vertebrates.

moral philosophy. The study of ethics. *See* ethics.

primates. The biological grouping, or order, of animals that includes species related to lemurs, monkeys, apes, and humans. Because humans are primates, people interested in animal protection are often especially concerned with how other primates (notably the great apes) are treated, since they share many characteristics with us. *See also* great apes.

primatocentrism. Favoring primates over other species, on the premise that primates are "higher" animals, and nonhuman primates are the most similar to humans. *See* speciesism.

reintroduction. The practice of returning members of species, such as wolves, into areas where they once lived but became extinct because of human actions. Reintroduction raises questions concerning the interests and rights of individuals versus species, and what, if anything, we are obliged to do to maintain biodiversity.

sentience. Awareness of pleasure and pain, emotions, and sense impressions. Both humans and other animals—including fish, worms, and insects—are sentient beings.

species. One of the basic biological groupings of living organisms having certain common attributes. Examples of species, using their Latin names, are *Homo sapiens* (human beings), *Canis lupus familiaris* (the domestic dog), and *Drosophilia melanogaster* (common fruit fly).

speciesism (pronounced *spee-sheez-ism*). A prejudicial attitude in which one judges others not on their individual characteristics but on their membership in a particular species or other biological grouping. Critics of this attitude use the term *speciesist (spee-sheez-ist)* for a person or an argument that takes this stance. An example of speciesism would be to view species in terms of a hierarchy—for example, claiming that vertebrates are "higher" than invertebrates, or that humans are "higher" than nonhuman primates like gorillas and chimpanzees. Many people would be willing to grant rights or special treatment to "higher" animals but not to "lower" animals. This book argues that such a hierarchy is not compatible with a philosophy of caring and sharing extended to all animals, for the good of the whole planet. Speciesism is also objectionable because it fails to take account of the value and needs of individual members of a species.

utilitarianism. A philosophy that makes moral decisions based on utility—the usefulness, benefit, or advantage of an action. In relation to animals, an action is considered permissible by utilitarians as long as the benefit to humans is greater than the cost to animals.

vertebrates. Animals with a backbone, or spinal column (vertebrae), which contains a central nervous system. Vertebrates include mammals, birds, fish, reptiles, and amphibians. *See also* invertebrates.

vivisection. The practice of cutting or operating on a live animal. The term can also refer to any invasive experimentation even if it does not include cutting.

welfarism. *See* animal welfare.

Index

Index